# LORD ABERDEEN AND THE AMERICAS

UNIVERSITY OF GEORGIA MONOGRAPHS, NO. 3

# Lord Aberdeen

# and the

# Americas

By

WILBUR DEVEREUX JONES

DEPARTMENT OF HISTORY

UNIVERSITY OF GEORGIA

UNIVERSITY OF GEORGIA PRESS
ATHENS                    1958

# Contents

v

# Preface

THIS monograph grew out of a number of my articles published in various scholarly history journals during the past several years. These articles dealt with certain specific problems in Anglo-American relations and were intended primarily to seek out and describe the motives which influenced the British statesmen in the diplomatic situations described. But they necessarily failed to present an over-all interpretive account of the Earl of Aberdeen's strategy in dealing with the nations of the New World.

Unfortunately, Aberdeen's able biographers, Sir Arthur Gordon and Lady Frances Balfour, do not stress his New World diplomacy. In fact, they ignore it almost completely. This is not strange—though it may seem so to Americans— for the Earl of Aberdeen, both as Foreign Secretary and later as Prime Minister, devoted most of his attention to Britain's relations with the nations of Europe, and it is quite natural that he should have done so a century ago.

This monograph is designed, therefore, to reconstruct that part of Aberdeen's story which has previously escaped attention. An effort is made especially to relate the diplomatic affairs of the New World during the period 1841-1846 to Aberdeen's fundamental policies. This study is confined to a discussion of those incidents in the Americas which point up and demonstrate Aberdeen's general policies, and does not, therefore, present a wholly complete account of Britain's relations with all the American nations during these years.

As this story has been derived almost completely from original sources, no bibliography is included. The references to the original sources will be found to include, first, the manuscript collection to which the source letter belongs, and second, its file number in that collection. Letters which do not include file numbers refer back to the first file number above them. The titles of various collections are abbreviated as follows: Aberdeen Papers (AP), Colonial Office Papers (COP), Gladstone Papers (GP), Peel Papers (PP), and the Ripon Papers (RP). All of these, except the Colonial Office Papers (at the Public Record Office), are housed in the British Museum.

This preface would not be complete without a grateful reference to Marjorie Lady Pentland. Lady Pentland, a descendant of the subject of this monograph, has always taken a keen interest in the proud history of her family, and thus it was particularly appropriate to submit this work to her for comments and criticism. Not only did she check the typescript carefully, but she allowed herself to be persuaded to write the charming and informative Foreword. It is with deep gratitude that I acknowledge her kindness.

The University of Georgia            Wilbur Devereux Jones
Athens, Georgia

# Foreword

WE in Britain have good reason to thank American scholars for all the study they have bestowed on many of the men and women who belong to our own history. By wide research and sympathetic understanding, Professor Wilbur Devereux Jones has now lighted up, as if on a television screen, the drama of British-American relations a little over a hundred years ago.

Through his skillful use of letters written by ministers as events unfolded we get a vivid picture of their background. They wrote on the eve of great changes. But their map of the American continent, with its various divisions and dominations, was still unbelievably different from today's. Then they could not guess at the wealth to be reaped from its wide lands, upon the surface and underground; communications across the Atlantic which now can be carried through in three minutes then might have taken three months. So men on the spot often had to act on their own judgment, for good or ill.

Professor Jones brings home to us the likeness as well as the contrast between that political scene and our own. We ourselves have seen the same countries and their leaders arguing over the same sort of questions. War preparations (including Congreve rockets, the forerunners of our guided missiles) and war action; claims about territories and boundaries by big powers; protests against "colonialism" and struggles for independence by small powers—these have been the anxieties of 1956-1957 as they were in 1841-1846. The light which Professor Jones has thrown on the past also reflects a warning for the present.

Naturally it has been a special pleasure to me, as Lord Aberdeen's great-granddaughter, to read this story of his success during his second term as Foreign Secretary. Evidently Britain owed much to his aims and efforts in avoiding a

# LORD ABERDEEN AND THE AMERICAS

fresh war with the United States while also drawing closer to France, both countries lately our enemies in battle. His biographers, thinking more about Europe and about him as Prime Minister of the Coalition Cabinet from 1852 to 1855, gave little space to his dealings with the West. Doubtless others will share my amazement on learning that his moderation kept him undazzled even by the idea of adding California to the British Empire.

Lord Aberdeen's own interests lay in art, archaeology, classical and European literature, foreign travel, and the improvement, planting, and beautifying of his Scottish estate. In later life he built himself a "Marine Villa" on the wild sea cliffs at Buchan Ness; over its door he engraved the words: *"Beatus ille qui procul negotiis"*—happy is he who is far from affairs.

From a child indeed he had known public affairs from inside, for he grew up among makers of British history. Because of the early death of his parents, he spent his boyhood in England, went to Harrow and Cambridge, and lived in turns with his two guardians, War Secretary Lord Melville and Prime Minister William Pitt. Under their auspices he mixed with the leaders in politics and in society of that day. An excellent actor (after he had received from Pitt an assurance that "Your character for attention to real Business cannot suffer from your taking a part in Amusement"), he often acted in amateur theatricals at Lord Abercorn's private theatre, where the brilliant company included such guests as Sir Walter Scott, the Sheridans, Lord Melbourne, John Philip Kemble, and Sir Thomas Lawrence.

In 1802, when he was eighteen, Lord Aberdeen went to Paris with a letter from Pitt to First Consul Buonaparte, who entertained him kindly at Malmaison and won his keen admiration. The young man proceeded through Europe to Greece where his researches earned Byron's description of him as "the travell'd thane, Athenian Aberdeen." The Government offered him diplomatic missions to Sicily, Russia, and the United States, which he refused because his lovely and adored young wife, Lord Abercorn's daughter, had become ill with consumption. After her death, however,

at Lord Castlereagh's pressing request, Lord Aberdeen went
in 1813 as special envoy to Austria during the Allied campaign against Napoleon. With Metternich, he rode across the
battlefield of Leipzig on the day after the victory; its sights
and sounds haunted him ever after with the horror of war.
Nor, though he married again later, could time efface
from his inner mind the memory of his loss when, after seven
years of perfect happiness, his first wife and her four
children had been taken from him by the same disease.
Always shy and sensitive after these blows, he hid his feelings
under a reticence which strangers took for haughty reserve.
Those who knew him best, whatever their shade of political
opinion, Queen Victoria, the Prince Consort, Wellington,
Peel, Guizot, regarded him with the greatest trust and affection. Lord Aberdeen was the first to offer a post in the
Government to young Gladstone, who long afterwards told
my father: "Among many statesmen for whom I have felt
respect and admiration, of your grandfather alone could I
say that I truly loved him."

My father, the late Lord Aberdeen, remembered him as
a grave but always indulgent grandfather. As a small boy
my father asked him for a cow (meaning, I suppose, an
ox) yoked together with a camel. After a search throughout
London, Lord Aberdeen reappeared at the Ranger's House,
Blackheath (where The Queen had given him the post of
Ranger), admitting failure but bringing a large toy camel and
cow separately. Another time the Prime Minister, as he
then was, walked up the path trundling a much-longed-for
small wheelbarrow. The head gardener, a stern man called
Basket, who always wore a tall hat while at work, one day
complained about damage done to the garden by the grand-
children. Whereupon Lord Aberdeen inquired: "Mr. Basket,
have *you* any children?"

"Yes, my lord, several," was the prompt reply, "and I
hope that your lordship can help my eldest son get into
the bank here as a clerk."

A glimpse of Lord Aberdeen in his Foreign Office days
was given soon after his death in 1860 by M. le Comte de
Jarnac in an article in the *Revue des Deux Mondes*. M. de

Jarnac recalled that soon after arriving in London as a young diplomat, in 1837, he noticed people respectfully saluting two gentlemen as they walked together toward the House of Lords. He inquired who they might be and a passer-by replied, with *laconisme national*: "Wellington and Aberdeen." M. de Jarnac particularly remembered Lord Aberdeen's kindly smile as he raised his finger to his hat in acknowledgment.

In 1843, as Counsellor to the French Embassy in London, M. de Jarnac posted up for talks with Lord Aberdeen at his home in Aberdeenshire (a five days' journey by *meilleure diligence*). Here at Haddo House, he wrote, *une nouvelle designation prit naissance* (a new expression was born), when Lord Aberdeen used the words "a cordial good understanding" to describe the relations he wanted between Great Britain and France. The phrase pleased M. Guizot and was adopted officially in 1844 when Louis Philippe, on a visit to Queen Victoria, spoke of the *entente cordiale* that should unite their countries.

Everyone who reads this paper will be able to imagine how much Lord Aberdeen would have liked to see not only two but all nations united in a cordial good understanding. I greatly appreciate the request of Professor Wilbur Devereux Jones that I should add this foreword, and on behalf of our family thank him for the thought and work which he has devoted to our ancestor's part in transatlantic affairs.

West Clandon, Guildford,                    Marjorie Pentland
October 12, 1957

## Chapter I

# In the Wake of Palmerston

On September 3, 1841 Lord Aberdeen accepted the seals of the Foreign Office in the Government of Sir Robert Peel. The situation was by no means new to him, for he had filled the position with distinction in the Government of the Duke of Wellington during the period 1828-1830, and his official connection with foreign affairs dated to the period of the Napoleonic Wars. But he could now approach his tasks with the added confidence which grew out of riper years and increased prestige in his own country.

Aberdeen knew, however, that he could not compete for popular favor with his predecessor, Lord Palmerston, who, during the past decade, had swept past one diplomatic crisis after another, and had frequently left his counterparts in other nations in clouds of bewilderment, chagrin, and often resentment. Palmerston's methods appealed to a generation deeply imbued with national feeling—a strong sense of national honor that was easily wounded and constantly demanded satisfaction for its hurts. Palmerston was an ideal physician to tend cases of injured national pride. Aberdeen, while he did not wholly lack this ability, preferred to base his diplomacy on less emotional foundations and chose to regard nations as entities with minds as well as hearts.

Palmerston's successes had, in fact, left behind a mountain of diplomatic problems. France, a nation whose good will Aberdeen had won in 1830 by the prompt recognition of the revolutionary government of Louis Philippe, was grievously offended by Palmerston's recent handling of the Eastern Question.[1] But France was not the only European nation hostile to Britain. The latter could, indeed, look down from

1

the lofty and lonely pinnacle of her European eminence upon a community of nations in which she scarcely had a reliable friend, save Portugal. Not all this hostility, of course, could be attributed directly to Palmerston, for it is the fate of nations in Britain's position to be jealously regarded. But the cavalier policies of the Viscount encouraged those who disliked England to do so more heartily.

Across the Atlantic the situation was hardly more promising. Upon the United States and Britain the Maine and Oregon boundary questions lay like deep-seated sores, and a more recent festering growth was the *Caroline* incident of 1837.[2] Even though the British law officers were uncertain regarding the legality of Britain's action in the latter affair, Palmerston turned a deaf ear to American demands for reparations and an apology. Then there was also the case of Alexander McLeod, still pending in a New York court. If McLeod were convicted and executed for his alleged complicity in the *Caroline* incident, Palmerston had threatened war against the United States.

Latin America likewise provided some knotty problems. In the La Plata region Uruguay, a nation Britain had helped bring into existence, was in a state of civil war, and much of its territory was occupied by Argentine troops. Then there was the problem of the Brazilian slave trade. Under the terms of recognizing Brazil in 1826, Britain had wrung a promise from her to end the slave trade, but Brazil made little effort to keep this promise, and British public opinion demanded some sort of action against her. Even more important was the question of Texas, which had won independence from Mexico, a fairly important British customer, in 1836. In 1840 Palmerston had signed a series of treaties with Texas, but they still remained to be ratified. The whole question of British relations with Mexico and the United States with respect to Texas was yet to be answered.

So, while Palmerston had established a considerable reputation for his handling of foreign affairs, he had left behind him many more problems than he had solved. Dealing with these questions was to occupy Lord Aberdeen for the next five years, to tax both his diplomatic skill and his patience

# REVIEW COPY

# UNIVERSITY OF GEORGIA PRESS

### ATHENS

TITLE:  Lord Aberdeen and the Americas

AUTHOR:  Wilbur D. Jones

PUBLICATION DATE:  April 21, 1958

PRICE:  $2.00

We would appreciate receiving two copies of your review.

to the utmost, and, in the end, to establish his place among Britain's illustrious Foreign Secretaries.

These many problems in foreign relations were, of course, not wholly left to Aberdeen, but to some extent concerned the whole Cabinet—especially the Duke of Wellington; Lord Stanley of the Colonial Office; the Earl of Ripon; and, of course, the Prime Minister, Sir Robert Peel. The Cabinet was bound together by a mutual admiration, if not in all cases affection, for Sir Robert Peel. Sir James Graham of the Home Office was probably Peel's most intimate friend; Aberdeen and Ripon thought very highly of the Premier. But Wellington and Stanley sometimes moved rather uneasily under the restraints of their political superior, who was socially their inferior.

Despite minor differences, Peel's Cabinet functioned smoothly, and one reason for this stemmed from the respect customarily accorded the opinions of each of its members. In minor matters Peel allowed his subordinates to run their departments, but on issues of importance, he was always consulted. His letters show that Peel never avoided or returned a vague answer to their questions, and much more than in his speeches is his brilliant mind revealed in these written replies. Peel's extraordinary insight into the ramifications of a problem at hand and his keen discernment of the various possibilities for its solution have been rarely equaled by national leaders of any age. The historian who reads hundreds of his letters never ceases to marvel at the superiority of his reasoning, and in his own time this quality captivated his colleagues.

But this does not cast a cloak of omniscience over Peel. In political affairs, and especially party politics, he was admirably well informed. In economic matters he was less so, and lacked the long experience of Lord Ripon. In questions of colonial policy Peel displayed little interest, unless Stanley (as occurred on occasion) found himself in difficulties. In foreign affairs the Prime Minister was considerably less informed than Aberdeen, or, for that matter, the Duke of Wellington.

This being the case, one might ask—how was foreign policy made in Peel's time? It is clear that, by and large, Lord Aberdeen was its architect. It was Aberdeen who laid down the broad outlines and objectives of foreign policy, though, when specific situations arose, other members of the Cabinet advanced their opinions, and these were given attention.

In moments of international tension when national defense was involved, both the Duke of Wellington and Lord Stanley had to be consulted. Stanley, an anti-imperialist and pacifist, usually followed Aberdeen's lead, but the Duke of Wellington sometimes caused difficulties. His position as head of the army naturally caused the Duke to think in terms of military requirements, and his status as a major national hero made him more sensitive of national honor than the others. Once formed, his opinions were usually tenaciously held. Unfortunately, given the same situation and the same facts concerning it, the Duke's recommendations frequently differed sharply from those of Aberdeen, who was not an army man.

In economic decisions Lord Ripon had a strong voice. Though Ripon had long since lost his political power, Peel never ceased to respect his economic views. In negotiating economic agreements with other nations, Ripon usually thought in terms of equivalents—that a British concession should be met by an equivalent concession on the part of the receiver. But Ripon was the most gentle and least dogmatic personality in the Cabinet, and he was ever ready to accommodate his views to the opinion of the majority.

Thus there were a number of individuals other than Lord Aberdeen who had a voice in various aspects of foreign affairs. Basically, however, there was a considerable homogeneity of outlook among the members of the Cabinet. Save for the Duke, none of these men was military minded. Peel or Graham might speak extravagantly on certain occasions, but these were the occasional deviations due to the winds and tides of politics and did not alter their basic course. Ripon once loved to study battles, but his real interest was in peaceful economic development. Stanley, an isolationist, believed other peoples should be allowed to follow their inclinations and follies unburdened by British intervention or advice.

Various outside factors, many economic in nature, influenced the Cabinet. Delegations from one company or another frequently called on Cabinet officials; petitions were presented with monotonous regularity in Parliament, and complaints from British interests abroad were received all too often. But economic policy did not mold foreign policy. It influenced foreign policy tactics, but it did not change the grand strategy.

Aberdeen himself had little interest in economic matters, even domestic ones, and once admitted he did not pretend to understand the issues involved in the much-mooted Corn Law controversy. Had he sought to blend economic and foreign policy, Aberdeen would certainly have interested himself in the numerous trade treaties projected by the Peel Government during 1841-1843. But on only one occasion did he intervene.[3] In shaping his foreign policy Aberdeen was influenced largely by history, by his Christian sense of right and wrong, and by the need of finding safety and friends for his country within a hostile community of nations.

Another outside factor which had some influence on foreign policy was the "blackguard newspapers." None of the Cabinet members had much respect for the press; one, Lord Stanley, feuded with the newspapers throughout his career. What Aberdeen resented most about the press was that it constantly fanned old prejudices and hatreds into flame, and thus increased the difficulty of burying old international enmities.

Public opinion was, of course, quickly reflected in Parliament, where the Opposition lay in wait to gain political advantage from it. Political parties then were less disciplined than they are now, and the voice of the mercantile section was particularly strong in shaping the courses of individual members of Parliament. Otherwise good Conservatives might be persuaded, on certain issues, to desert their party, and thus cause it grievous embarrassment. But, when not stirred up by the press, the rank and file of the Conservative Party was psychologically in agreement with Aberdeen's type of leadership. The Conservative Party still drew most of its nourishment from the land, especially the country squires, and they were inclined to be much more concerned with corn averages than Britain's relations with the far-off nations. If prices were good, they were satisfied, even smug, and inclined to expect little from less fortunate nations.

If the activities of the mercantile section and the press acted to restrict Aberdeen's freedom of movement, so certainly did the question of slavery. Britain at this time took great pride in her opposition to that institution, an attitude in tune with the general moralistic outlook of the budding Victorian Age. While the Whig Party had accomplished the emancipation of the slaves in the British Empire, the Conservative Party had afterwards absorbed the two men most closely identified with that act—Lord Stanley and Lord Ripon—and hence had a large stake in continuing the fight.

This policy, while supported with enthusiasm in Britain, presented Aberdeen with one of his most annoying issues abroad.[4] Especially in dealing with the Americas did Aberdeen find himself involved with vexed questions arising out of slavery and the slave trade, and, though it is often charged that Britain derived benefits from her anti-slavery crusade, the Cabinet did not seem to have been very much aware of these benefits. In their correspondence among themselves on slavery, the Cabinet members invariably considered the subject from a lofty, humanitarian standpoint.

So Aberdeen's problems in 1841 were many and varied, and to some extent he was not a free agent in dealing with them. He had to strive for unanimity in the Cabinet, which was often most difficult to obtain. He was bombarded by private business interests who demanded policies to promote their own affairs. He was harassed by the press, which constantly opened old international wounds, and by the Opposition in Parliament which naturally sought issues to advance their political prospects. He was forced (though not against his will) to carry on the anti-slavery crusade even though it might disturb his basic policies. Aberdeen, however, had the gift of patience, an important quality for the successful diplomat, and he was not disturbed when he had to proceed but slowly through the maze.

\* \* \* \* \*

The cornerstone of Aberdeen's foreign policy was the establishment of an *entente cordiale* with France. Even before Melbourne's Government left office the prospective Peel Cabinet had agreed that peace with France was possible, and had decided to act with her in a spirit of friendship. This was apparent during the debate on the Address in August, 1841, when Ripon spoke in favor of friendly relations with France, and Peel referred warmly to Guizot.

In holding out the possibility of ending the traditional hostility between France and England, Lord Aberdeen was not merely indulging in wishful thinking. King Louis Philippe was most favorably disposed toward peace, and toward Aberdeen personally. His minister, Guizot, while French ambassador in London, had come to know and like Aberdeen. Aberdeen was convinced of their good intentions, but he feared the French Opposition, led by Thiers, who had been recently alienated by Palmerston, and certain extremist factions in the French legislature who constantly clamored against Britain. Thus, while Guizot might promise many things, Aberdeen had always to estimate the value of his statements in the light of the political situation in France at the moment.

Aberdeen's colleagues were less optimistic in 1841 regarding the possibility of establishing friendly relations with the United States. Until the McLeod case was settled, no step could be taken in that direction, but there were cogent reasons why an attempt should be made as soon as possible. Aberdeen not only regarded friendly relations with the United States as desirable in itself, but felt that Anglo-American friendship would promote a cordial tie between Britain and France. Peel and Ripon, who thought in terms of exports and imports, found an added incentive toward this goal in America's value as a customer of Britain.

The first major problem to come to Aberdeen's attention, however, did not directly involve France or the United States, but Texas. In November 1840, Palmerston had negotiated a commercial treaty with Texas, as well as others, providing for British mediation to end the state of war between Mexico and Texas, and for the suppression of the slave trade. These treaties had been negotiated by General James Hamilton, the Minister Plenipotentiary of Texas, but they had not yet been ratified by either nation.

Hamilton, who now had to convince the Peel Government of the worth of his projects, secured an introductory letter to Lord Aberdeen from Lord Ashburton, to whom he had previously been recommended by Henry Clay. He made a favorable impression on both Peel and Aberdeen when he met with them in September. But since many of his proposals were of an economic nature, they were turned over to Lord Ripon for his opinion.

There were four major parts to his proposals. In exchange for a treaty of commerce which would give Britain preferential tariff rates, and a treaty which would permit Britain to search Texas' ships in the suppression of the slave trade, Hamilton sought a guaranteed loan of £1,500,000. Ripon, in his reply, attached some importance to both of the concessions offered by Hamilton, and considered the security for the loan—timber, land, and "the whole revenue of the State"—to be fairly adequate. But, in general, his letter lacked enthusiasm.

A fourth proposal Ripon vetoed very firmly. "I ought to add that I would have nothing to do with that part of his project which refers to a part of the public debt owed to British subjects," he wrote. "It has always been thought right not to encourage British subjects to lend money to Foreign States, & if the Texas Govrnt. bind themselves to pay that debt by Treaty, we shall be bound to see that they do so; which might be very embarrassing."[6] He was referring here to one of Hamilton's favorite proposals—that, in exchange for Texas paying off $5,000,000 of the Mexican debt owed to British bondholders, Britain should try to secure Mexican recognition of the independence of Texas and a favorable boundary settlement.

Though Hamilton sent a number of importunate letters to Aberdeen, and presented a large number of reasons why Britain should interest herself in the affairs of Texas, Aberdeen was unwilling to go beyond the treaties already negotiated by

Palmerston. So the moment passed without action.[7] This does not indicate, however, that Aberdeen was hostile toward Texas and partial toward Mexico. In the autumn of 1841 he was primarily interested in his plan to establish cordial relations with the United States, and he evidently had not decided yet just how Texas would fit into his general strategy.

So this "Very last invented Empire of Texas," as Ashburton called the new nation, had to wait until the larger diplomatic picture had been clarified, and until Aberdeen could integrate his Old World policy with the flow of events across the sea.

CHAPTER II

# A Boundary for Maine

VARIOUS members of the Peel Government had watched with concern the growth of the Anglo-American crisis of 1841. In May, Wellington thought war was probable, and in August, Graham urged that the consideration of relations with the United States be given priority.[1] Nothing, however, could be done that summer, for the McLeod case was still pending in New York, and in October Peel was considering "some immediate and decisive demonstration" against the United States.[2]

When, on October 12, 1841, a New York court found McLeod innocent, the diplomatic skies cleared considerably, and Aberdeen immediately began to sound out his colleagues regarding questions still outstanding between Britain and the United States. This was difficult to do, for autumn usually found the landed aristocrats of the Cabinet scattered, resting at their various estates and engaging in social amenities. And it is questionable that Aberdeen tried very hard to secure their definite opinions at this stage of his project, for too set a program might work against his idea and simply prove that a major negotiated settlement with the United States was impossible. In November the *Creole* incident arose to complicate further the situation.[3]

So the groundwork for the mission to America—a mission which he hoped would improve relations with France as well as with America—was laid by Aberdeen with the advice of Peel and Edward Everett, American minister in London, who was a close friend of Aberdeen. His talks with Everett and the reports of Henry S. Fox, the British minister at Washington, convinced Aberdeen that the United States was

10

in a mood to negotiate. Needed to assure the success of the project was a British negotiator who stood well with the Conservative Party, and who was known to be friendly with the United States. Henry S. Fox had few friends in America, and therefore was felt to be unsuited to the task.

Alexander, First Lord Ashburton, head of the financial house of Baring, filled both requirements; so Aberdeen conferred with him early in December. Ashburton, somewhat reluctant, accepted when Aberdeen assured him that his mission would be favorably received in America. No doubt Aberdeen also emphasized his own willingness to compromise the issues in dispute and neglected to mention that these views might not have the support of the Cabinet.[4] He urged that Ashburton leave before Parliament met, and Ashburton, for domestic reasons, was anxious to depart. Aberdeen drew up his instructions with the approval only of Sir Robert Peel,[5] and the mission departed with considerable haste.

While Aberdeen and Ashburton hoped to adjust most of the problems outstanding between the United States and Britain, both realized that the success or failure of the mission would be determined by the outcome of the Maine boundary negotiations. Aberdeen hoped that the boundary could be adjusted on the basis of the arbitration Award of the King of the Netherlands in 1831, which had been rejected by the American Senate by a rather close vote. Aberdeen favored this Award not because it gave specific advantages to Britain, but because it was the disinterested finding of a third party and hence could be easily defended in Parliament. He was privately contemptuous of the area involved. ". . . I must declare," he wrote, "that if we shall at last be driven to quarrel with the United States, I sincerely pray that we may take our stand on some great principle of national policy, or of humanity and justice; and that we may not go to war for a few miles more or less of a miserable pine swamp."[6] As we shall see, there was more in this statement than applied to Maine.

Feeling as he did, Aberdeen did not secure the opinion of the Duke of Wellington regarding Maine until Ashburton was about to depart. The Duke's memorandum on the subject rejected the Award of the King of the Netherlands, and supported the extreme British claim in Maine.[7] It arrived at a most inconvenient time, for Ashburton still had an opportunity to back out. So, in sending the memorandum to Ashburton, Aberdeen minimized its importance, noting: "If the Duke's views were to be adhered to, you would have little chance of success, but at the same time they deserve attention."[8] Privately he noted: "It will be necessary for the Cabinet, at a very early date, to consider what modifications of the Instructions may be advisable, in consequence of the Memorandum."[9] Later, on receiving the revision of his instructions due to the Duke's memorandum, Ashburton noted that, he would have considered it "inexpedient" to go to America had he known of the contemplated revisions before he left. Aberdeen's tactic, therefore, probably saved the project from being stillborn.

During the Cabinet discussions on Maine the two main themes were the defense of Canada, and achieving a settlement which would be favorably regarded in Canada and Parliament. On February 24, 1842 Aberdeen addressed a communication to several British military authorities requesting their views on the disputed territory with respect to the defense of Canada. Their replies were contradictory, but that of Sir James Kempt, who wished "to retain the whole country between the Right bank of the St. Lawrence, and the South West Branch of the St. Johns River," received particular attention.

After these discussions and inquiries, Aberdeen's private letters to Ashburton did not stress a military road or economic advantages in the disputed area, but rather a settlement which would look well on the map. This is clear from the following excerpts from Aberdeen's letters:[10]

I believe it [the territory north and west of the St. John River] is a mere swamp, not even producing timber of any value, and offering no temptation of any kind to Settlers. Still, however, to look at the Map, and to find that we have acquiesced in bringing Inhabitants, by possibility, of the United States within sight of Quebec, would scarcely be tolerated in this country.

My belief is that it will be preferable for us to give up

everything to the South of the St. John, & to retain the District between the St. John & the St. Lawrence, in consequence of the appearance of bringing the Americans so near to Quebec.

But Ashburton was mainly interested in securing the Madawaska Settlement along the St. John River, and he continued to fight unsuccessfuly for that area even after he had received Aberdeen's revised instructions.

The details of the negotiations between Webster and Ashburton are told in many places.[11] It need simply be noted here that Aberdeen, in his private letters, offered concession after concession in an effort to secure the area described above, which was, incidentally, also that sought by the Duke. He was willing to give up a small area on the Connecticut River, to make a money payment to the United States, to give the Americans the right to float timber down the St. John, and, finally, under certain conditions to cede some purely British territory called the "Narrow Strip," which was not even involved in the dispute. When Ashburton advised him that certain bribes had been distributed, Aberdeen replied: "In order to ensure success, you need not be afraid of employing the same means to a greater extent in any quarter where it may be necessary."[12]

Toward the end of the negotiations Aberdeen penned a paragraph which gave Ashburton authority to do almost anything:[13]

I only wish to say that the importance of a successful result is so great, as almost to justify any sacrifice compatible with the safety of the North American Provinces. . . . It is too late now to enter into elaborate argument, for any useful purpose. The matter will be settled by you, while we are engaged in discussion here.

Perhaps Aberdeen's willingness to make concessions in the Maine boundary controversy was increased by his gradual realization that Ashburton could not settle the minor problems. Aberdeen could not renounce the practice of impressment (though he assured Ashburton in a private letter that it would never be renewed, and the latter no doubt gave this information to the American Government), nor could he give guarantees that incidents such as the *Creole* would not occur again in the future (though for a time Aberdeen apparently hoped such slaves might be classed as mutineers and returned to the United States). The Law Officers insisted on maintaining the indelibility of British nationality, and refused to consider slaves as coming under the laws of mutiny. On the other hand, Aberdeen permitted a round-about apology for the *Caroline* incident, though officially it was merely an explanation.

When Ashburton returned home, Aberdeen recorded his private opinion of the final treaty:[14]

> As throughout . . . I have written to you with perfect frankness, I will now say that the only part of the negotiation which causes me any regret is the abandonment of the Upper part of the St. John, as the boundary. . . . although in point of value the difference is unimportant, the effect here would have been considerable. I am not certain that, failing to obtain the whole line of the St. John, it might not have been preferable, for the sake of the impression to be produced, to have adhered without alteration to the Award of the King of the Netherlands in all its parts. I have said, however, that I am perfectly satisfied; and this is really the case. It is only with the view of being enabled more effectively to resist a popular ground of attack that I would have wished for any change. The good temper in which you left them all, and the prospect of a continued peace, with, I trust, improved friendly relations, far outweigh in my mind the value of any additional extent of Pine Swamp.

As a reward for his services Aberdeen offered Ashburton the title of viscount and the Order of the Bath, but the latter was not interested in either of these honors.

The aftermath of the treaty was not wholly favorable to the Government. Palmerston launched a bitter attack in Parliament, but he did not enlist support. As for the British attitude in general, Ashburton wrote: ". . . though my Treaty has been approved by all but Palmerston, nobody viewed it very thankfully & most people were disposed to shake hands with him [Brother Jonathan] rather sulkily."[15] Two years later there was still some discussion of the *Caroline* apology, and, on receiving a letter from Ashburton in which he advocated firmness, Peel observed: "Advice from *Ash-*

*burton* about *nailing Colours to the Masts* is rather amusing.
I wish he could see my pending controversy with Sir James
Head about his *apology*."[16]

There can be no question but that the Ashburton mission
was successful, though the degree of its success is not easily
determined. Ashburton believed that a "collision" would have
shortly followed the failure of the mission, and, if this is so,
then its importance is very great because it prevented a
useless war. However, the mission fell far short of establishing
a lasting cordial relationship between the two nations.

This was quite evident during the early part of 1842,
for, while the United States Government was negotiating
with Britain in Washington, some American ministers abroad
were striving to undermine Aberdeen's policy in France. In
December 1841 Aberdeen had sponsored the Quintuple
Treaty, which provided reciprocal rights of search among
Britain, France, Russia, and Austria in an effort to put down
the slave trade. Due partly to the activities of the American
minister in France, Lewis Cass, the French legislature post-
poned ratification of the treaty, and, indeed, did not accept it
until 1845. Aberdeen had hoped that Ashburton's success
would cut down American anti-British activities in France,
but he realized this might well be wishful thinking.

Aberdeen, in fact, was in a puzzling position. He desired
peace and friendship with both France and the United States.
But was such a three-cornered friendship possible, especially
when the United States and France had been allied against
Britain in two wars? Reduced to a geometric pattern, Britain
was the apex point of a triangle with a short base, and
France and the United States were the other two corners,
much closer to each other than they were to Britain. There
was obviously only one thing for the apex to do in this
situation—to quietly push itself downward toward the other
two points, which in the process must be spread farther and
farther apart!

This is the departure in Aberdeen's foreign policy that
has been overlooked. It is the explanation for his attitude
toward Texas, which, in the past, has puzzled many historians
who have sought to clarify his motives.

As was noted above, Lord Palmerston had negotiated a series of treaties with Texas in 1840, and they still remained to be ratified. Britain was slow to take action, but so was Texas, and one need not find in this situation any evidence of British hostility toward Texas, or favoritism toward Mexico. A memorandum in the Peel collection states briefly that Britain in this case followed her usual practice in cases where treaties required the ratification of foreign legislatures—she simply waited until the Texas Congress took action.[17] Britain, in fact, anticipated ratification by appointing Charles Elliot her Consul-General for Texas on May 31, 1842.

Ratifications were finally exchanged in the Foreign Office by Aberdeen for Britain and Ashbel Smith, Texan Chargé d'Affaires in London, for Texas on June 27, 1842. Included were treaties for Amity, Commerce and Navigation, another for the Mutual Suppression of the African Slave Trade, and a third for British Mediation with Mexico. The second, even though it was not too effective in form, was unpopular in Texas, but she had to accept it with the others. The failure of the Quintuple Treaty made Aberdeen particularly keen to have the slave trade treaty signed, and it was also useful to him because it placed British relations with Texas on a high humanitarian plane.

The immediate aftermath of the recognition was to place officially before Lord Aberdeen the question of the *Montezuma* and *Guadalupe*, two ships built for the Mexican service under contract from the Mexican Consul, Lizardi.[18] Ashbel Smith protested Britain's fitting these ships with armaments, and carried on a lengthy correspondence with Lord Aberdeen through the summer. At least one well-known authority on Anglo-Texan relations interprets Aberdeen's failure to prevent the outfitting of these ships as evidence of Aberdeen's alleged partiality toward Mexico at this time.[19] Ashbel Smith insisted that Aberdeen might intervene under the terms of the Foreign Enlistment Act; the latter denied it. The most Aberdeen could do was to prevent the ships from leaving British ports with armaments aboard, and to threaten to take away the commissions of British officers who manned vessels for Mexico in combat service. Smith was not convinced, even though his Home Government did not consider the incident as a breach of British neutrality.[20] A similar vexed question was to arise during the Civil War in the case of the Laird rams.

Of more importance to Anglo-Texan relations than these ships was the mediation problem. In March 1842 the Mexicans had made a fairly successful foray into Texan territory, and there was an excellent prospect of further attacks. Texan authorities, who probably exaggerated British influence over the Mexican Government at this time, felt that British mediation would be a logical means of halting future Mexican aggression.

On July 1, 1842 Aberdeen sent a dispatch to his representative in Mexico instructing him to tell Mexico that it was Britain's "earnest desire" that she should make peace with Texas, and to stress that at the present moment "decidedly advantageous" terms might be had. By this phrase he probably meant that Texas might be persuaded to accept the purely nominal sovereignty of Mexico. Such a solution would probably accomplish a project dear to the hearts of the British Conservatives—the abolition of slavery in Texas. The advice of Britain, however, was rejected by the Mexican Government, and the refusal was reported in a dispatch of August 29, 1842.

Ashbel Smith concluded that Aberdeen was not really aiding Texas, and he sought to explain the British attitude to the Home Government. In June he advised his superiors that Britain was interested in Texas mainly as a barrier against American expansion and as a source of cotton, and noted that Britain avoided steps that might offend Mexico, a good customer which might be an ally in a future war against the United States.[21]

While there is some substance of truth in Smith's interpretation, it should not be taken at face value. Britain's interest in Texas was actually very slight. While Texas might provide cotton for hungry British mills, this was something still in the future, and though Texas was, indeed, a barrier to American westward expansion, Britain regarded her rather as a bulwark against the complete absorption of Mexico by the United States. Aberdeen at this moment could hardly have put much stock in Mexico as an ally, for, due to the Ashburton mission, Anglo-American relations were unusually good. Finally, while it is true that Mexico was a fairly good customer of Britain's and there was possibly a $50,000,000 British investment there, Mexico's political instability discouraged investment, and at this time Britain was losing much of the Mexican trade to France and Germany.[22]

This does not mean that Smith's observations were wholly erroneous. But it does mean that to emphasize these factors is to obscure the outlines of Aberdeen's foreign policy. If Aberdeen were inactive in Texas early in 1842, the main reason for his inactivity was his inability to fit his Texas policy into his over-all strategy. As a matter of fact, Aberdeen had meager information regarding Texas at this time, and the reports he received were often so conflicting that it was difficult to form sound conclusions. For this reason, Charles Elliot was sent to Texas with instructions to report privately on conditions there as soon as possible.

To Aberdeen's annoyance, Elliot's private report did not reach England until the late autumn of 1842. It was, however, reasonably complete. He discussed in some detail the population of Texas, where her people were settled, the problem of the southern frontier, the quality and quantity of Texas' cotton production in the future, and the functioning of the government. Elliot reported favorably regarding the energetic nature of the people and the production of cotton, but his description of the government was not encouraging: "As yet the criminal law is a dead letter; there is no land force; the marine is either dismantled and going to ruin or locked up at New Orleans for want of funds. There are no means in the Treasury, and I am concerned to say that the legislative proceedings concerning the finance of this Republic have been unwise and unjust."[23]

On the basis of this report the most that Aberdeen could conclude was that the future of the new republic was very uncertain.

Following his modest success in adjusting differences with the United States, Aberdeen in 1842 began to devote increasing attention to building an *entente* with France. Such a project would be aided immensely if the two nations could be brought to cooperate and to act as a unit in the solution of one or more important international problems. Just at that time there were two major areas for such cooperation—Texas and the La Plata region.

Aberdeen approached the La Plata problem with considerable hesitation. Britain had commercial interests there; so did France. The continuing war between Buenos Aires and Montevideo hurt commerce and caused a demand in both countries for governmental intervention to achieve an armistice. Thus, the La Plata seemed to offer an excellent opportunity for Anglo-French cooperation. One major consideration, however, caused Aberdeen to hesitate—the region was so remote that it was extremely difficult to supervise intelligently the work of diplomatic agents there. By the time news of a given situation in the La Plata region arrived in England and instructions were drawn up and sent back, the situation would be likely to have changed considerably.

Nevertheless, Aberdeen could not afford to overlook this possibility for Anglo-French cooperation. That summer Britain and France instructed their ministers in the La Plata region to make "most urgent" representations to Buenos Aires and Uruguay to end the war, and to demand that the former's troops be withdrawn from the latter's territory. These demands were accordingly made on December 26, 1842, but they were virtually ignored. The British and French ministers, exceeding their instructions, went on to threaten the use of a naval force to secure their objectives.

When the news of their activities finally arrived in England, Aberdeen drew back. While it was heartening—and, indeed, a minor success for his policy—to have France and Britain acting together in that region, he was not ready to become involved in naval or military operations. So he more or less shelved the project for two years.

Meanwhile the diplomatic situation with respect to Texas and Mexico became increasingly complex. Aberdeen was advised of the failure of his offer of mediation in a dispatch received in England on October 14. Pakenham, the British minister in Mexico, reported: "Mexico maintains her obstinacy in rejecting any agreement with Texas; and will not entertain the mediation of Great Britain offered by Lord Aberdeen. This is in a measure owing to Santa Anna's existence depending on a milatary [sic] Govt. for power, and to the necessity to him of having a field wherein to exercise it."[24] Information was also received that the Mexicans planned a vigorous prosecution of the war during the spring of 1843.

The idea of mediation, however, did not die. Ashbel Smith had received instructions from his Home Government to try to interest Britain, France, and the United States in a triple mediation. As both Britain and the United States had already offered to mediate, his problem was to interest France in the project.

It proved to be impossible to bring the three nations to agree regarding the terms of their mediation. Aberdeen hoped that Texas might accept the "nominal sovereignty" of Mexico as the price of its virtual independence. This would prevent the annexation of Texas to the United States, and perhaps help bring the extinction of slavery in Texas. The United States, however, could not accept this suggestion. Richard Pakenham reported from Mexico on December 25, 1842 as follows:[25]

The French minister has received no instructions regarding the proposed triple mediation of France, England and the United States, and Mr. [Waddy] Thompson affirms in a conversation with Mr. P[akenham] that it is impossible his Govt. can admit the reconquest of Texas by Mexico, since Emancipation must follow, wh. wd. have an injurious and dangerous effect on the slave states of the Union adjoining.

Thus the position of the United States in opposition to any attempt to settle the Texas problem by re-establishing the authority of Mexico over her was thus made clear.

Even before this information was received Aberdeen had advised Smith through a subordinate that Britain would not act with the United States in a triple mediation, and intimated that Britain preferred to act alone.[26] The official reason given for this refusal to act with the United States was the unfriendly relations then existing between that nation and Mexico. But it seems clear that Aberdeen did not want to act alone. He desired to secure the cooperation of France, but in the autumn of 1842 a major attack was taking shape on Guizot's government, and the debates were expected to have an anti-British tone. Thus the moment was not right for Anglo-French mediation.

During 1842 Aberdeen sought to convince Mexico that a settlement of the Texas problem was highly desirable. In July he had instructed Pakenham to advise Mexico that so long as the present situation continued Mexico would be embroiled with the United States, and further: "The Mexican Govt. ought not to suppose they can at any time obtain succor from Great Britain in their struggles in Texas or with the United States. Great Britain has determined to remain quite neutral."[27]

On the other hand, he apparently hoped that the gathering threat of a Mexican invasion might cause Texas to accept a compromise solution with regard to her independence. Early in December 1842 Aberdeen wrote Elliot:[28]

. . . the hostile operations of the Mexicans appear to have acquired additional vigour, and may be attended with some effect; but I am persuaded that anything like conquest of the Country is as improbable as ever. We shall do all in our power to bring them to a more conciliatory policy notwithstanding our mediation has been refused; and I have some reason to hope that it will not be very long before a change shall take place in this respect.

The precise grounds upon which Aberdeen based his hope that Mexico might change her attitude are not clear. Possibly he was referring to a projected trade treaty between the United States and Texas, which might convince Mexico that annexation was near.

That winter Aberdeen was able to coordinate his policy in Texas with that of France. So the two nations once again were able to act with some degree of unity toward the solution of a major diplomatic problem. Under date of February 24, 1843 Pakenham reported from Mexico:[29]

The Baron de Cyprey has recd. instructions from Mon. Guizot in every way conformable with those of Ld. Aberdeen, respecting the settlement of difficulties between Mexico and Texas. The success lately obtained agt. Texas makes the Mexican Govt. desirous of another *expedition* and thus no hope can be entertained of an pacification.

About a month later Pakenham sent another dispatch, as follows: [30]

Reports conversation with General Santa Anna, who is willing to come to some agreement with Texas upon certain conditions wh. illness prevented him from putting on paper. Mr. Pakenham is of opinion that there is a large party in Texas favourable to a junction again with Mexico, and that ere long Texas will belong to the United States of Mexico.

With this prediction Pakenham left his post in Mexico and later that year went to Washington. He was replaced as Chargé to Mexico by Percy W. Doyle. Looking ahead, the wholly erroneous conclusion he reached regarding Texan affairs was certainly a poor recommendation for a man shortly to undertake the delicate Oregon boundary negotiations with the United States. As we shall see, his conduct of those negotiations was less than satisfactory.

Percy Doyle was evidently advised by Aberdeen to do what he could to prevent a renewal of the Mexican raids on Texas. This, at least, is the theme of his first private letter to Aberdeen. He wondered if he might not induce British seamen in the Mexican service to refuse to participate in raids on Texas. But he feared that if they should refuse the Mexican Government might ask him to intercede with the men, and this would put him in an embarrassing situation, after secretly urging them not to serve.[31] Doyle, incidentally, displayed little knowledge of Mexican affairs, and tended to lean on the advice of Elliot in Texas.

Whatever plans for joint action Aberdeen may have had in mind early in 1843 were complicated by a project undertaken by Santa Anna at the same time. In February he released a prisoner, James W. Robinson, who returned to Texas with the offer of an armistice. As the price of the armistice, Santa Anna demanded that Texas again become a department of Mexico with autonomy rather than inde-

pendence. Pakenham evidently did not learn of Santa Anna's
project until March, but it is evident that he encouraged the
Mexican caudillo to believe Texas would accept these conditions.

His successor, Doyle, was drawn into the project in May.
Pakenham reported: [32]

> In an interview with Santa Anna, he declared to Mr. Doyle
> his willingness to bring about an adjustment of the differences
> between Mexico and Texas, and that he had submitted his terms
> through a Texian (Mr. Robinson) to General Houston at the
> same time declaring his readiness to receive commissioners and
> negotiate with them on the terms mentioned in Capt. Elliot's
> desps. and also to maintain an armistice, of wh. he authorizes Mr.
> Doyle to make General Houston acquainted with.

Doyle relayed this information to Elliot on May 27, 1843.
"I trust I may not have erred in giving my assistance to the
Proclamation of the Armistice," he wrote Aberdeen privately.
"I did not see that any harm could arise from it. . . ."[33]
Thus the two British ministers, in Mexico and Texas, ap-
parently acting largely on their own initiative, achieved a
minor success designed to forestall further Mexican raids
on the territory of Texas.

While President Houston of Texas could not possibly
accept the terms offered by Santa Anna, he nevertheless
declared the armistice on June 13, 1843. It, of course, did
not provide the basis for peace between the two countries,
and, insofar as Britain was concerned, the incident merely
led to a tiff between Elliot and Doyle. Doyle explained it
to Aberdeen as follows: [34]

> In a letter which I received at the same time with the Pro-
> clamation from Captain Elliot, I find that he thinks I expressed
> too strongly an opinion of his with respect to a large Party in
> Texas being willing to accept the terms offered them by Presi-
> dent St. Anna. I took this opinion from a passage in a letter
> to me which ran thus: "It would certainly not surprise me to
> find this project temporarily favoured, and perhaps it would not
> be hard for its advocates to show them that General St. Anna's
> scheme would be as profitable an arrangement for Texas and the
> United States as I am sure it would be a mischievous one for

Mexico." I regret My Lord very much if I have stated too strongly what Captain Elliot intended.

On the basis of this statement, it appears that Doyle, like Pakenham before him, encouraged Santa Anna in this project; at the same time Elliot was trying to convince the Texans that Doyle was endeavoring to induce Santa Anna to give up all claims of sovereignty over Texas.[35]

This second British intervention in Mexican-Texan affairs has all the earmarks of lack of planning. It resulted from Elliot's and Doyle's initiative as they sought to adapt their general instructions to the march of unexpected events. Aberdeen's hand does not show itself in the documents, for, despite the fact that French and British policies in Texas were being coordinated early in 1843, we do not find the French ministers acting with Elliot and Doyle. So this incident does not fit into the scheme of grand strategy which Aberdeen was developing.

CHAPTER III

# Aberdeen's Strategy at High Noon

INSOFAR as Anglo-American relations were concerned, the first year of Aberdeen's administration of foreign affairs had been reasonably successful, but it was obvious that the Ashburton mission had left many problems unsolved. To many in the Cabinet the American tariff of August 1842 came as a disappointment, for Britain suddenly faced a tariff wall against her cotton goods amounting to 120%, and another against silk goods of 90-100%. In 1845 Lord Clarendon estimated that British merchants had lost almost a million dollars as a result of the tariff up to that time.[1]

The line adopted by President Tyler in his special message of August 11 and in his annual message of December 6, 1842 regarding the nature of the cruising convention signed by the two countries provided another irritant. "Nothing can be more wholly false or insincere," Ashburton wrote, "than the President's insinuations on this subject. . . ."[2] He denied that the convention was in any sense a substitute for the "right of visit," carried out by British cruisers in the suppression of the slave trade, and insisted that Webster and Tyler had considered Aberdeen's note on this subject wholly satisfactory.

Ashburton, indeed, was somewhat dissatisfied with the outcome of his mission, and he was in this mood when the United States began to sound out Britain on the subject of another comprehensive agreement, this time to include the Oregon boundary, a commercial treaty, and the possible American acquisition of Upper California from Mexico. Regarding the last of these, which is particularly interesting, the private correspondence offers no enlightenment. Britain

25

had already investigated the condition of California late in 1841 and found it to be wholly defenseless.[3] About the same time Pakenham sent the Home Government a plan whereby an otherwise unidentified "Company of Adventurers" would occupy Upper California, establish a sovereignty there, and then appeal for the protection of the Crown. Lord Stanley, to whom the communication was referred, replied he "is not anxious for the formation of new and distant colonies, all of which involve heavy direct and still heavier indirect expenditure, besides multiplying the liabilities of misunderstandings and collisions with the Foreign Powers."[4] Later Aberdeen told Peel there were "many projects" regarding California submitted to the Government during these years, but neither he nor Stanley encouraged them.

That no commercial treaty with the United States was attempted at this time was probably due to Peel. In April 1843 Peel sent to Lord Ripon a private letter which Webster had written to Everett on the subject of a trade treaty, noting that unless there was definite assurance of its success a treaty had best not be undertaken. He added:[5]

The power of the United States Senate to reject a Commercial Treaty, and the miserable motives of personal resentment and party interest by which men in the United States are influenced occasionally in deciding on the gravest Questions of public Concern make Caution and Reserve doubly necessary.

Lord Ripon's reply could not be found among his papers.

But in rejecting the American overtures at this time the Government was guided by Lord Ashburton. A paragraph from one of his letters is particularly enlightening:[6]

Webster's exact position would require a longer story than you might like to read. He cannot remain Secretary of State, and not knowing how otherwise to dispose of himself, he is desirous of getting up for himself a special mission to this country, which Everett evidently does not like. The ostensible objects of this mission are—The Columbia River Boundary—and a commercial treaty—by which last is meant a renewal of the controversy respecting the colonial trade which some years ago were treated by Huskisson with no inconsiderable acrimony. If Webster comes here we cannot help it, but I would not recommend giving it any encouragement, for the party at Washington will give him restricted powers, what he does, whether right or wrong, will not have much chance of ratification by the Senate. . . . My recommendation would therefore decidedly be to prefer if possible treating these or any other matters with Everett on whose candour & honesty I have the very best opinion. When Webster leaves the President, the latter is likely to fall into the hands of Cass and a Mr. Cushing. Both very bad men for us. The latter if anything the worse of the two, because much the more able. . . .

His basic objection to the mission, then, was his belief that Webster was powerless to do good.

Regarding the Oregon question, Ashburton told Aberdeen that Webster and he had discussed it, but he shortly discovered that the only line permitted by his instructions would be unacceptable to Webster. "I believed him on this subject," wrote Ashburton, "to stand in awe of the two Missouri Senators, who afterward voted against the whole treaty."[7] In another letter he explained further this subject:[8]

It would undoubtedly be desirable to settle the Columbia river Boundary. I am not sure that Webster did not keep open this question with me as an excuse for his coming here, but at the same time I feel confident that I could have done nothing that the Senate would have ratified within the limits of my instructions. Everett has communicated some suggestions on this point which, if they satisfy you, might I think be made to work. These give up the mouth of the Columbia River & run a line from below Vancouver to the Straits of Juan de Fuca. If anybody had power to negotiate to this effect the settlement might be worth the sacrifice we might make; but if we are not careful we run a risk, in the present state of parties, of making the concession without obtaining our Treaty. I have a bad opinion of the good faith of the party likely to be in power. . . .

This letter is highly important because the compromise suggested (while not very definitely described) seems to be the one finally accepted. Of considerable importance are the last two sentences, which indicate why the British Government (which leaned heavily on Ashburton's authority regarding affairs in the United States) hesitated to suggest such a compromise at this time.

Following Ashburton's suggestion, Aberdeen sought to learn the views of Everett on the Oregon question, and, if the American Government had seen fit to give him powers to arrive at a compromise solution, the major crisis which developed later would have been forestalled. Under the circumstances Aberdeen decided to transfer the site of the Oregon negotiations to Washington, where the British negotiator would be in closer touch with American political developments. Everett, who was deeply interested in preventing the development of a crisis, urged that Aberdeen convey the news of his decision by the mail of November 4, 1843, so that it would arrive before the President delivered his annual message to Congress.[9]

Perhaps to avoid a partisan charge that he was "truckling" to the United States, Aberdeen decided against sending another special mission to Washington. But, even if he had desired to do so, Ashburton would not have undertaken it.[10] He therefore advised Richard Pakenham on October 7 that he would be sent to the United States as minister, with special instructions to settle the Oregon question. At the same time Aberdeen assured him this employment was temporary, and that an effort would be made to find him a post in Europe.[11]

The choice of a man who had so wrongly judged the situation in Texas did not bode well for the future, but Aberdeen seems to have had considerable confidence in Pakenham's abilities. It was almost a month later (but in time to catch the mail of November 4) that Aberdeen advised Fox of his replacement:[12]

It has been thought desirable, and indeed necessary, that this [the Oregon Question] should be treated at Washington, and not in London, as had formerly been proposed. There is too much reason to apprehend that your Relations with the American Govt. are not such as to contribute to the prospect of a happy result. We cannot send another special Mission; and under these circumstances, it has been thought expedient for the publick service that your place at Washington should be supplied by Mr. Pakenham.

Thus it is clear that Aberdeen did his best to lay the foundations for an amicable settlement of the Oregon question.

As in the case of Maine, Aberdeen was slow to draw up the instructions for his representative, and also as in that case, he was not impressed by the value of the territory to be divided. Likewise, as in Maine, Aberdeen preferred to have the matter settled by arbitration, for this would tend to remove it from party political considerations in both countries. But he had little hope that the United States would accept this solution. Nevertheless, in his instructions to Pakenham arbitration was one alternative; the other was even more unacceptable to the United States—the Columbia River boundary. In drawing them up, Aberdeen consulted only Peel, probably because he did not want to risk receiving another of the Duke's memorandums such as complicated the Maine boundary negotiations.

No doubt Aberdeen had little hope that either of these suggestions would be accepted, for he had talked the matter over carefully with Everett in the autumn of 1843. As we have seen, Ashburton had informed him of a more acceptable compromise earlier that year, and Everett in his talks with Aberdeen no doubt suggested extending the 49th degree parallel only to the sea, leaving Britain in possession of Vancouver Island.[13] But this suggestion had not been made officially and Aberdeen, following Ashburton's advice that a concession made too readily might result only in weakening Britain's position, was cautious. On March 4, 1844 Aberdeen wrote Pakenham privately:[14]

It is very likely, however, that you will not be long, when once you open the negotiation, before you are to the end of your concessions and that these will fail to prove sufficiently acceptable to the U. S. Govt. to lead to a settlement of the question. . . . I confess myself not to be very sanguine in the expectation that you will have brought Mr. Calhoun to accept our terms. Should my apprehension be verified, you will endeavour, without committing yourself or your Govt. to draw from the American Negotiator a proposal to make the 49th degree of latitude the boundary, with the proviso that all Ports to the South of that parallel to the Columbia inclusive shall be free ports to Grt. Britain. The navigation of the River Columbia shall be common to both; and care should be taken that the 49th degree of latitude, as a boundary, is to extend only to *the Sea*; and not to apply to Vancouver's Island. Without actually committing us, I think you might give them reason to hope that such a proposal would be favourably considered.

When he made this suggestion Aberdeen, insofar as is known, had not yet consulted anyone in the Cabinet, but he advised Peel of his opinion in the autumn of 1844.[15] In so doing, Aberdeen officially identified himself with the Everett compromise.

Thus we know that Aberdeen himself was ready to sign what was to be the final settlement in Oregon at least as early as September 1844, if not in March, and that Pakenham had been authorized to "draw from" the United States such an offer. We know also that Everett had informed American Secretary of State Abel P. Upshur late in 1843 that Aberdeen would probably accept the offer.[16] Why, then, were the negotiations so protracted?

According to an authoritative account of the negotiations in Washington, when Pakenham took up the discussion with John C. Calhoun he was told that it would be impossible for the United States to accept anything less than the 49th parallel—that the Senate would refuse to ratify a less favorable treaty.[17] This, then, would explain in part why Britain did not formally offer the compromise suggested by Everett— it would become merely the stepping stone to a capitulation, not a compromise.

On the basis of these facts, it would appear that the mighty argument in Washington during 1844-1846 did not concern the territory between the Columbia River and the extreme 54-40 degree latitude, or even the territory between the Columbia River and the 49th degree parallel, but ultimately only Vancouver Island, the navigation of the Columbia River, and the other minor points at issue. Aberdeen feared to offer the Everett compromise lest it be rejected and he be left with nothing; Calhoun (assuming that he was in possession of the information Everett sent to Upshur) would not offer the Everett compromise because he did not think it would pass the Senate.

Viewed in these terms the Oregon dispute, about which so much has been written, settles down to a petty quarrel which reflects little credit on the diplomatic services of either of the great nations involved.

Meanwhile in 1843 the *entente cordiale* had entered upon its most prosperous phase. Louis Philippe delighted the French bourgeoisie with his attentions to their welfare, and Guizot, through the astute use of his patronage powers, had a fairly stable majority in the legislature. Queen Victoria and Prince Albert in September 1843 helped consolidate Anglo-French friendship by visiting Louis Philippe. Although a few clouds were forming in Tahiti, Greece, and Spain to eventually dampen the *entente cordiale,* these were not very evident at the moment and the sun shone brightly.

It was in this atmosphere that Aberdeen's grand strategy for Texas was nourished. During the summer of 1843 a party of American and Texan abolitionists met in London, and Aberdeen was approached with a plan to have Britain buy out the slaveholders of Texas.[18] Though he was aware that such a plan would be regarded as a hostile act by the United States, Aberdeen, who opposed slavery everywhere, went along with it, and for a time did his best to induce Mexico to make emancipation a condition for the recognition of Texan independence. The project only served to deepen American distrust regarding British intentions.[19]

The year 1843 produced many incidents which served to point up the corruption and ineptitude of the Mexican Government. Doyle explained:[20]

> Your Lordship can hardly imagine the daily complaints I am obliged to bring before this Government made by British Merchants in all parts of the country. . . . The difficulties we meet with here arise greatly from the disordered state of the Treasury. The Minister of Finance told me a few days since he had not a single dollar to pay even the Garrison of Mexico. This state of penury arises very much from the malversation which goes on from the highest to the lowest. They therefore seize upon any money they can lay hold of, taking their chance of being obliged to refund it hereafter.

At times, as in the case of the Copper Decree,[21] Santa Anna manipulated public finances to benefit himself and his friends, and foreigners often suffered thereby.

This need for money gave rise to an extraordinary incident, which, if Doyle's account of it be accurate, was indeed a prize piece of chicanery. He charged that Santa Anna was interested in provoking an international "incident"; so he invited Doyle to a public dinner at which was displayed a captured British flag. Doyle demanded its removal, and when this was refused he suspended all normal intercourse with the dictator. Santa Anna therefore found it "necessary" to station a large body of troops near his palace. It was very convenient to have the soldiers around during the election then in progress. Furthermore he was able to sell a large number of his own cattle at high prices to his Government to feed the soldiers. Once the resulting tension had fully served his election and economic purposes, Santa Anna blamed the affair on his Minister of War, General José M. Tornel.[22]

Lord Aberdeen watched with some concern the distracted state of Mexico, and was annoyed with Doyle, who served as interim representative following the departure of Pakenham, for having broken relations with Santa Anna over such a minor matter. On November 11, 1843 he advised the able Charles Bankhead, who had long been interested in the Mexican post, of his appointment to it. Some time during this period, if not before, Aberdeen laid plans for his most daring diplomatic venture.

As we have seen, the close friendship between France and the United States was more than a source of annoyance to Britain. It was a continuing danger. France was a great land power; the United States had shown in the War of 1812 the ability to inflict enormous losses on British shipping.[23] During 1841-1843 Britain had been on strained terms one time or another with both France and the United States, and Aberdeen had had to worry about the possibility of a two-front war. The Cabinet always had to ask—if we fight France, what will the United States do? And—if we fight the United States, what will France do? Even in peaceful times, the ill-will the Americans stirred up in France against Britain was very inconvenient. If the traditional friendly relationship of these two countries could be broken, it would indeed be a grand stroke for Britain.

The Texas question offered an opportunity to cement the *entente cordiale*, and to force France to choose between the United States and Britain. France had long evinced an interest in Texas and Mexico, and, though her economic interests in those areas were much smaller than those of Britain, she was at least mildly opposed to further American expansion into the Southwest and West. If Britain were able to bring a diplomatic clash between France and the United States in Texas, the traditional Franco-American alliance would receive a telling blow. This is the background necessary for understanding Aberdeen's famous "Diplomatic Act" of 1844.

There are a number of excellent accounts of the background and development of this act. One of these, based on the materials then available, is found in Justin H. Smith's work on the annexation of Texas.[24] According to Smith, Aberdeen was convinced that President Sam Houston of Texas desired to maintain the independence of Texas, and the American Presidential Message of December 1843 (though it contained nothing regarding annexation) together with a dispatch from Elliot, revealing that the United States had plans to annex Texas, turned Aberdeen's thoughts toward intervention.

Thereafter communications took place among Aberdeen, Guizot, and Ashbel Smith, and the first two decided they would issue a joint protest against the contemplated annexation. But by the time instructions to this effect had been sent to the British and French ministers in the United States, Calhoun had already signed an annexation treaty (April 12, 1844). Aberdeen and Guizot then decided that a mere protest would not only be ineffectual, but might actually cause American public opinion to consolidate behind the annexation scheme. Aberdeen, however, anticipated that the political situation in the United States would not permit annexation at that time.

Looking beyond the momentary failure of the annexation scheme, Aberdeen on May 28 or 29, 1844 called in the Mexican minister in London, William S. Murphy, for an interview. He told Murphy that if France agreed and Mexico would recognize the independence of Texas, Britain would unite with France not only in guaranteeing the independence of Texas, but would also guarantee the Mexican boundary. He further promised that Britain, under these circumstances, would "go to the last extremity" in opposing the annexation of Texas. Following the interview Aberdeen advised his minister in Mexico of the project, and indicated that if France would agree they might take "further measures" to force Mexican compliance, if that state still refused to recognize Texas.

For some reason not clear to Justin Smith, Aberdeen did not formally reveal his plan to Ashbel Smith until June 24, 1844, but the project seemed to be going on smoothly. France was prepared to sign the act. Sam Houston sent written instructions to Anson Jones, his Secretary of State, to conclude the bargain. But just at this time Anson Jones became president-elect, and he chose to disregard the instruction.

On July 18, 1844 Aberdeen decided to postpone the measure to "a more fitting season." As it turned out, the season did not become more "fitting." In France opposition to cooperation with Britain grew, and Guizot became lukewarm toward the project. The dismal end of the plan came on October 23, when Aberdeen advised Mexico that her failure to recognize Texas relieved Britain and France of any further responsibility under the terms of the projected act. Thus Mexican reluctance to recognize Texas, Anson Jones' failure to accept the act, and the lukewarmness of France doomed the Diplomatic Act.

What conclusion did Smith draw from this sequence of events? ". . . it is perfectly clear," he wrote, "that Great Britain was so anxious to prevent annexation that she was ready, if supported as her minister indicated, to undertake a war in order to establish at the Sabine [River] a perpetual barrier between us."[25] He concluded that Britain was ready to fight not only the United States, but also Mexico, if necessary to secure her compliance. Another eminent authority on this subject, E. D. Adams, concluded: "Aberdeen practically announced his willingness to go to the point of war with the United States," but adds, in defense of the peace-loving Aberdeen: "Aberdeen . . . never seriously thought that war would result."[26]

Being perhaps the most interesting single development in the story of Aberdeen's diplomacy with respect to the Americas, the Diplomatic Act deserves the closest study. Unfortunately this sequence of events noted above took place during the session of Parliament, and hence the plans for the act were laid at regular cabinet sessions. This writer could find only the following sentence in the *Peel* and *Aberdeen Papers* written at the time of the project—"I hope," Peel noted, "you are preparing the groundwork for the defiance of the United States in respect to Texian annexation."[27] This would seem to confirm that strong action was anticipated.

Retrospective references to the act made by Aberdeen the following year are somewhat conflicting. He observed that France "began well, but timidly, in Texas. . . ."[28] On another occasion, however, he commented: "In the case of Texas and the river Plate, they [the French] have done exactly what we desired, and in the manner in which we desired it."[29] Putting these two observations together, it would seem that British policy was much bolder than that of France with regard to the annexation question, but that Aberdeen was satisfied with France's role in the project.

Did Aberdeen contemplate the possibility of a war with the United States in 1944? Evidently he did. Even more in those days than today a competent foreign minister had to bring his nation to the "brink of war" to accomplish important national policies. The national policy here involved was of very great importance, for it envisaged a diplomatic revolution involving not only France and Britain but also France and the United States. To cement the *entente cordiale*, and to destroy the Franco-American friendship, Aberdeen could feel perfectly justified in going to the "brink of war." These were the important considerations in Aberdeen's mind—not the value of an independent Texas.[30]

But this does not mean that Aberdeen either wanted or expected war. He set in motion a series of events whose end he could not possibly foresee, but he probably hoped the project would result in acrimonious exchanges, especially between France and the United States. No preparations were made for war by Britain; in fact, the evidence is to the contrary.[31] The mere fact that he mentioned the "last extremity" to Murphy does not mean that he anticipated war. Aberdeen saw in this strong language the only means of securing Mexico's recognition of Texas, but at the same time he placed a number of qualifying phrases in the agreement which would allow him to escape if he wished to do so.[32]

The alleged readiness of Aberdeen to go to war with Mexico may be regarded in much the same light. He made it clear that Texas must forswear forever the idea of uniting with Mexico as a permanent settlement. To induce her to accept such terms, Aberdeen had to speak strongly, and hence indicated that Mexico would be "forced to submit" to their decisions. In this way Aberdeen tested the good faith of certain Texans who maintained that they desired independence above all other solutions. When Anson Jones refused to accede to these terms, Aberdeen was undoubtedly convinced that Mexican recognition of Texan independence would probably be merely the first step toward annexation by the United States. If, of course, the Texans actually desired to be independent, then Britain would be perfectly justified in aiding them to establish and maintain their independence, providing they asked for such aid.

To speculate upon the consequences of the Diplomatic Act had it been successful leads one down the interesting but endless road of what might have been. What Aberdeen would have done we can only postulate upon the basis of what we know of his character; and knowing he hated war, we must concede that war would have been a last resort. With respect to Mexico, Aberdeen possibly planned some sort of coercion such as will be described in the next chapter in his dealings with Buenos Aires. An Anglo-French war with the United States would certainly have changed the traditional alignments, but this drastic measure would have smashed that part of his foreign policy designed to improve Anglo-American relations, and the triangular relationship mentioned earlier would have been distorted into a fantastic shape.

It is a mistake, however, to conclude that the Diplomatic Act was a failure. On the one hand, England and France had united temporarily in a major diplomatic venture, and, on the other, Aberdeen had aroused in the United States some dissatisfaction and suspicion of France. In the process, of course, Anglo-American relations were disturbed, but the other two considerations overbalanced the third.

----------

Far from planning a war against the United States, Great Britain in the autumn of 1844 was fearful of American preparations, especially in the Great Lakes region. Aberdeen remonstrated with the United States Government in June 1844 for her alleged violation of the Rush-Bagot Agreement of 1817, but he had to be satisfied with an evasive reply. While the Cabinet discussed the possibilities of erecting land fortifications to defend Canada, Aberdeen, who loathed the doctrine of *bellum para, pacem habebis,* combined with the peace-loving Stanley and the budget-minded Peel to prevent any steps from being taken.[33]

The storm that broke over Anglo-French relations during the summer of 1844 probably would have prevented the success of the Diplomatic Act even if all other factors had been favorable. It was the more serious because it sprang from a number of sources. Early that summer the Prince of Joinville, the third son of Louis Philippe, published a pamphlet on French naval affairs and discussed with undiplomatic candor the possibilities of raiding British coastal towns. About the same time French activities on the Moroccan frontier, following the suppression of the Abd-el-Kader rebellion in Algeria, caused suspicion of French aggressive intentions in North Africa. But the major "incident" arose in the Pacific area, where Britain had offended France in 1840 by taking over New Zealand.

The Tahiti incident had its roots in the competition of the French Catholic and British Protestant missionaries in that island. When the latter won over the Queen of Tahiti, the Catholic missionaries secured the intervention of the French navy, and France announced that the island had been taken under her protection in September 1842. Later the Queen tried to repudiate this agreement, and the Protestant leader attempted to regain his position. Finally there was a clash, and several French sailors were killed. For this the Protestant leader was imprisoned. Though he was later released and indemnified the incident created a sensation on both sides of the Channel, and Peel—in his role of defender of the Protestant Church—late in July 1844 made a most intemperate attack on France in the House of Commons.

Peel's letter to Aberdeen of August 21, 1844 not only indicates the seriousness of the situation existing between France and Britain, but also underlines the dilemma of Britain's situation with respect to the United States:[34]

> I would most earnestly advise that we should without delay consider the state of our Naval preparations as compared with that of France. Matters are in that state that the interval of 24 hours—some act of violence for which the French Ministry is not strong enough to make reparation or disavowal—may not only dissipate the shadow of the *entente cordiale*, but change our relations from Peace to War.
>
> ... Let us be prepared for War. ... The first Naval Engagement may determine the question whether we are to contend at Sea with France single-handed, or whether the United States will declare in favour of France against us. It may also materially influence the decisions of the Northern Powers of Europe.

Thus it appeared that war—"the greatest of all calamities," Aberdeen called it[35]—was not far off. But Aberdeen was determined not to let it occur, and he refused to take preparedness measures which might create a war psychology. "There is no more false maxim," he replied bluntly to Peel, "as applied to Great States, than that we ought to prepare for war, in order to preserve peace. A Small State may perhaps arm for its defence, & to prevent war. A Great State can only prepare for war, in order to make war."[36]

Aberdeen and Guizot prevented war at this time. They had, in fact, determined to resign on the same day if the mob psychology of their respective nations brought on war, and together they managed to keep the peace. But the *entente cordiale* was further strained by events in Greece, where the British minister was building his country's prestige at the expense of France. Guizot protested his activities to Aberdeen in October 1844, and the latter reprimanded his ambitious underling. This event, however, tended to prolong the war scare in Britain.

In November 1844 the Ordnance Office drew up a report on Malta fortifications which chilled both Peel and Stanley.[37] But this was merely one facet of Wellington's general plan to establish new defenses in the Channel islands, Gibraltar, and other places. When these plans were sent to Aberdeen in December, the Foreign Secretary angrily protested a plan "which would virtually stultify our whole policy for the last three years," especially at this time of "profound peace." He continued:[38]

At a time, too, when the King of the French comes boldly forward, and proclaims his defiance of the war party, by publickly avowing that his whole policy is founded on the continuance of an intimate friendship with England. I believe this policy to be shared by all the most influential men in France. It is not upon the administration of M. Guizot alone that we may expect to find proofs of a desire to cultivate the Alliance with this Country. I have very recently received intimations of a similar desire on the part of Count Molé & M. Thiers. Why, then, should we incur an enormous expense, & create general distrust, at such a moment, when there is no reason to apprehend any danger. . . . During the late discussions relating to the events in the Pacifick, there never was any chance for war. Our friendly relations might have been interrupted, which would have been a great misfortune, and a state of coolness might have succeeded to a cordial understanding; but the possibility of war for such a provocation, was quite out of the question.

The last two sentences, of course, refer to his own state of mind, not the collective mind of the Cabinet. Aberdeen continued his remonstrances into the new year. ". . . we must not forget," he urged, "that we have lately had proof in two very important affairs of the entire concurrence of the French in our views, and that they have literally prepared their instructions at our dictation. In the cases of Texas and the river Plate, they have done exactly what we desired, and in the manner in which we desired it."[39]

Thus the diplomacy in the New World was called in by Aberdeen as a means of serving that in the Old.

CHAPTER IV

# La Plata: Threads Entangled

IN 1842 Lord Aberdeen had enlisted the cooperation of
France in an endeavor to settle the long-standing disputes between Montevideo and Buenos Aires. French and British ministers in the area had taken the intervention all too seriously.
The naval threat they held out to the contestants was not approved by the governments of France and Britain, and the
intervention was a total failure. Aberdeen, however, was not
allowed to forget the situation. In 1846 he said that not a
month went by thereafter without his being charged with
neglecting British economic interests in the La Plata area.[1]

The attempt at mediation in 1842 had had the support
of Brazil, and that country also continued to interest herself
in the situation to the south. British relations with Brazil
were rather uncertain. On coming to office the Conservatives found that steps were being taken to renew a commercial treaty with Brazil, and that a quarrel existed regarding
the terms of the old one. Brazil claimed that the treaty was
scheduled to expire in 1842, but Britain insisted that a two
years' notice was necessary prior to its expiration, so that
it would actually not lapse until 1844.

Another question which muddled Anglo-Brazilian relations was the slave trade. In 1826 Britain had helped secure
Brazilian recognition abroad in exchange for Brazil's promise
to abolish the trade in Negro slaves. In 1831 Brazil unen-
thusiastically passed a law to curtail the trade, but it went
unenforced and the transport of slaves actually increased
rather than declined. Britain was disturbed at Brazilian at-
tempts to evade their obligations, and one part of the Webster-
Ashburton Treaty called for a joint remonstrance by the
two English-speaking nations to both Brazil and Spain.

40

"Your remonstrance to Brazil & Spain is good," Aberdeen
assured Ashburton, "and you are right in taking it for granted
that you cannot go too far in that direction."[2] The United
States, however, did little to live up to the agreement.

As the Conservatives undertook to negotiate a new commercial treaty with Brazil, the slave trade abolition arose to
cause complications. "If we are to make a concession in
favour of Brazilian Sugar & Coffee," Lord Ripon wrote
Gladstone, "it must be in return for some stringent & really
efficient regulation on their part in respect to slave trading &
even slavery."[3] One plan was to force the freeing of slaves
held by British subjects in Brazil.

Two other major considerations further complicated the
negotiation of this treaty. If a major tariff concession were
made to Brazil with respect to sugar, it would put slave-
grown sugar in competition with the free-grown sugar of
the British West Indies. Quite as important was the state
of the national revenue—the sugar duty was one of the
largest income-producers in the entire British budget. All
of these factors combined to make the negotiation very
difficult.

But at length Ripon's relative, Henry Ellis, led a special
mission to Brazil to negotiate the treaty. The attitude of
Britain toward Brazil at this time was far from being generous.
Within a few months it was quite apparent that no treaty
would be made, and Ripon frankly traced the failure to
England's badgering Brazil on the subject of the slave trade
and to her having nothing "tempting" to propose.[4]

Brazil was not very interested in the economic offers of
Britain, but she continued to hope for her intervention in the
La Plata region. Late in the summer of 1843, Brazil sounded
out the British minister at Rio on the subject, indicating that
she was interested in cooperating with England in the project.
About the same time a letter describing this offer was received
by Aberdeen, a representative from Montevideo arrived in
England, and he promised "every kind" of concession in
return for British protection.

Aberdeen decided to consult with France, and wrote
Peel that he thought both France and Brazil should be

included if Britain decided to intervene.[5] Peel agreed that a "joint demonstration" might be made, but suggested that Aberdeen consult Wellington on the subject.[6] The following day Aberdeen wrote Peel again, noting ". . . the desire for our interference is almost universal here."[7]

But Aberdeen did not encourage the project in 1843. In fact, he resisted it, and, as we have seen, chose to intervene in Texas instead. This is another instance of his placing pure diplomacy ahead of economic considerations. As it turned out, this seemed to be a most fortunate decision, for no sooner had the Diplomatic Act fallen through and the war scare with France run itself out than once again Brazil brought up the matter of the La Plata. It seemed like an excellent opportunity to rescue the foundering *entente*. When Aberdeen learned that Viscount Abrantes of Brazil planned to stop in England shortly en route to Berlin, he seized the opportunity immediately. "This may perhaps give us facility in adopting with France a policy of interference," Aberdeen wrote Peel, "but our relations with Brazil are likely to become unpleasant and complicated."[8]

It is obvious that Aberdeen's course with respect to Brazil at this time was circuitous. It was necessary that a Latin American nation should invite Anglo-French intervention, for otherwise the European interference might seem arbitrary. Brazil had brought the problem to Britain; she must now place it before the French Government. Once Brazil had fulfilled these functions, she might thereafter be quietly ignored. Aberdeen, in fact, did not trust her. "The opening may perhaps afford some facility for the restoration of peace between Buenos Ayres & Monte Video," he observed. "We must be careful, however, not to encourage the Brazilians in any project of recovering possession of Monte Video, which I should not be surprised if they had in view."[9]

Although Aberdeen had long resisted the pressure of the British community to intervene in the La Plata region, once he made up his mind to do so he stepped forth determinedly. He had to assume that mere words might not end the war, so he inquired among the army and navy officers regarding the probable effect of a naval "demonstration" and a blockade in bringing Rosas, the Argentine dictator, to terms. Only one officer warned that these means would probably not be effective, and his opinion was therefore disregarded.[10]

As Aberdeen was not sure "how far the French Govt. may be inclined to act with us in this matter,"[11] he took a very strong line during his interview with Brazil's Viscount Abrantes, much the same as he had done with the Mexican minister in May 1844. We do not have a minute of this interview, but the impression received by Abrantes was as follows:[12]

Vict. Abrantes stated that nothing could be more satisfactory than his interview with your Lordship . . . that Lord Aberdeen he understood to accept frankly & without reserve all the contingencies and consequences of armed intervention (war if necessary in any possible form) . . . .

So Abrantes could go to Paris full of enthusiasm and perform his necessary function of enlisting France in the intervention.

Abrantes proposed to Guizot that the French and British provide 1,200 troops to supplement the 10,000 or 12,000 man army furnished by Brazil. But he found Guizot evasive and unenthusiastic. An even greater shock awaited him when Abrantes learned from the British minister in Paris that Aberdeen would not engage "in a continental war in S. America."[13] Thus the promise (or impression, we cannot be sure which) Aberdeen gave Abrantes was wholly repudiated a month later. Once Brazil had served the function of bringing France and Britain together, she was none-too-politely eased out of the picture. When William Gore Ouseley was sent on his special mission, he was specifically instructed to have nothing to do with Brazil.[14]

Another crisis in the French Government caused some delay, and William Gore Ouseley, who had been selected as the special British minister to Buenos Aires to mediate the war, waited in Paris until the situation cleared. His instructions were both verbal and written. Regarding the verbal instructions, we have the following information supplied by Aberdeen himself:[15]

I entertained some hope of an amicable settlement with Rosas, if it could be effected before the arrival of the French Minister at Buenos Ayres, for there were many reasons which might have induced him to come to an agreement with us. Unfortunately the French Minister arrived so soon after Ouseley that there was not time for our separate negotiation to succeed, & when once united, I never thought it possible for Rosas to yield, except to coercion.

What a far cry from the pugnacious plan Aberdeen revealed to Abrantes! What a far cry, indeed, even from the stern impression Aberdeen was giving to France of his intentions!

Officially Ouseley was instructed to go to Buenos Aires to persuade Rosas to withdraw his troops from Uruguay, then to induce both Oribe and Fructuoso Rivera to give up their pretensions to the presidency of Uruguay and to hold a free election to decide between them. If Rosas refused to withdraw his troops and raise his blockade by a "certain day," British and French naval squadrons were to effect these objects by force. While "H. M.'s Government have no intention of carrying on any operation whatever by land . . .," the combined forces were to seize Martin Garcia or any other place necessary for their security, or to make their operations "effective." Ouseley might also call for sufficient forces to protect British subjects, should they be in danger. These steps were to be taken in close collaboration with France.

Since the explanation of the above verbal instructions was written later, after it was obvious that peaceful mediation was impossible, we might be justified in regarding it as an apocryphal excuse to justify a failure. But we know that Ouseley first tried to accomplish his mission singly; so it is obvious that Aberdeen, perhaps fearing excessive demands by the French, hoped that a major diplomatic success could be achieved without resort to arms. France would be permitted to share in the credit, but the actual terms of the agreement with Rosas would be made by Britain. It was a rather singular means of laying the basis for the success of the *entente cordiale*, but it was consistent with the wishes of a man truly devoted to peace.

Ouseley arrived at Rio de Janeiro in April 1845, where he found the Brazilian Government not unnaturally in "high dudgeon" at their exclusion from the venture. But much more disturbing was the report he received of the activities of the American minister at Buenos Aires, William Brent, Jr. "Mr. Brent," Ouseley reported indignantly, ". . . has been influenced by Rosas & his entourage (it is said) and protests against any intervention by European Governments in Amn. affairs—making any interference a *casus belli*."[16] Thus the Monroe Doctrine—the "American System," Rosas was to call it later—arose to vastly complicate Ouseley's mission.

To counteract Brent's influence, Ouseley, who was generally friendly toward the United States, appealed to the American minister at Brazil, Henry S. Wise, and secured from him a letter to Brent (to be delivered by Ouseley) designed to prevent his "further compromising his Govt. or himself."[17] Ouseley also wrote a letter to Pakenham in Washington in which he noted: "I forgot to say that I am informed that the Govt. of Buenos Ayres has so far imposed upon poor Mr. Dent's [*sic*] credulity as to make him believe that the French or English have agreed to colonize or take possession of some part of the Banda Oriental! etc. etc."[18] He sent this letter through the American legation, hoping the "Philistines" would open it and thus be assured of Britain's true intentions. Later Aberdeen gave further assurance to the American Government that Britain was not bent on seizing the area.

The damage, however, was done. When Ouseley reached Buenos Aires his chance for a *sub rosa* settlement with Rosas was gone, and the dictator constantly referred to the "American System." "The very name of intervention," Ouseley reported regretfully, "or even 'friendly mediation' is hateful to Rosas."[19] True to the verbal instructions, however, Ouseley sought to accomplish his mission on his own, and wrote Aberdeen that he had endeavored to give his French colleague, Baron Deffaudis, employment at Montevideo for a few days. "He is quite welcome," Ouseley added, "but he may I fear be apt to use coercion unnecessarily, & claim credit for 'his thunder'."[20]

Ouseley negotiated with Rosas through a third party, and secured a vague promise that the dictator would recognize the independence of Uruguay and withdraw his troops if his candidate for the Uruguayan presidency, Oribe, should be given possession of Montevideo and allowed to serve out his term. Ouseley probably would have accepted these terms, if they had been made officially, but, as he feared, Deffaudis would not desert Rivera, whom France had supported since 1838, and the project fell through.

Thereafter the position of Ouseley and Deffaudis at Buenos Aires became increasingly uncomfortable, even dangerous. Anti-foreign demonstrations were held, and Rosas aroused the infamous *mazorca* club into bloody acts against the British. Ouseley offered a large reward to informers in an effort to circumscribe the activities of that organization, but he was compelled to report fifteen murders. The interventionists were relieved of their unpleasant situation when their ultimatum to Rosas to withdraw his troops from Uruguay expired on July 21, 1845. Amid cries of *"muera los Ingles,"* they fled to Montevideo.

The situation there was far from encouraging. The city was defended by an unruly group of irregulars and was teeming with Oribe's agents and spies. Supplies had to be brought in from Rio de Janeiro at such great expense that Ouseley became nervous over the drafts he made upon the British Exchequer. Oribe's forces controlled the entire hinterland and were camped within five miles of the city. The navy sent by Britain to aid Ouseley was composed of ships too large for use in those waters and "lie in the mud half their time 3 or 4 miles off."[21]

For a time Ouseley hoped that he might be able to bribe the Argentine forces supporting Oribe ("the cheapest way after all," he wrote), but they proved less venal than he hoped and the project failed.[22] Deffaudis, who was anxious to return to what he considered a civilized section of the world, favored strong action. He had his way and the combined operations began in late summer.

The opening rounds were easily won by the interventionists. The Argentine fleet blockading Uruguay was captured; the island of Martin Garcia, which controlled the Uruguayan coast, was taken without a fight. Colonia, which was to be used as a point of rendezvous for the combined fleets, had to be captured in order to blockade Buenos Aires. This, however, was not seized without bloodshed, and Montevidean forces (Ouseley thought it wise to use them instead of Europeans) clashed with those of Oribe. On September 18, 1845 the interventionists announced the blockade of Buenos Aires.[23] Far from bringing Rosas to heel, these measures simply complicated matters for the interventionists, and increased their supply difficulties. Even before the blockade had been announced, Ouseley had reached an advanced point in his thinking with regard to the situation in La Plata. On September 8 he wrote privately:[24]

We must not conceal from ourselves the gravity of the position, the whole of the Coast of Buenos Ayres and all of the Banda Oriental shut to us. It is from opening the Rivers that we can alone expect any advantage. General Paz occupies Corrientes—and were that Province and Entre Rios, and Paraguay (which Rosas claims as his own) supported in opposing General Rosas, we might either force him to acquiesce in the Terms proposed by the French and English Governments, or succeed in overthrowing him entirely and this would be the better result.

Ouseley retired that night in a thoughtful frame of mind, and woke at three in the morning to pen a most belligerent private letter:[25]

A better system than that of continuing to blockade and carrying on indirect hostilities, would be to declare war against Rosas (not the Argentines) at once, and thus do away with the equivocal position that gives a handle for misrepresentations of acts of coercion.

He demanded more serviceable ships, hollow shot, field pieces, and Congreve rockets—"these latter being unknown here . . . would be most useful." Deffaudis had already promised to secure some French troops; so Ouseley requested some British marines. All of this was necessary, he argued, if they were to accomplish the purposes of the intervention.

In contemplation since early August was a plan to send

an expedition up the Parana River to "liberate" the merchandise detained inland. At a time when he thought this move would be approved by his Home Government, Ouseley took credit for originating it, but afterwards he tried to trace it to Deffaudis.[26] As the French had undertaken a similar expedition in a previous intervention, neither of the ministers apparently anticipated opposition from their superiors.

The expedition began on November 17, 1845, and at the time Ouseley was ignorant of the fact that Rosas had been fortifying a position at Obligado ever since he learned of Abrantes' mission to Europe. On land were "4 formidable batteries, with chains [Frigate cables] across the River supported on 24 or 26 vessels—dismantled brigs, schooners etc., etc,. the guns 36, 32, 28, 24. . . ." as well as some 3,000 troops. To stiffen the last of these a cordon of 2,000 cavalry was thrown around the whole position. ". . . Rosas," Ouseley explained with chagrin, "has plenty of Congreve Rockets & other modern inventions *of which we have none*."[27]

Beginning at ten o'clock in the morning, the battle continued until seven at night. The batteries, chains, and boats were destroyed, and a large supply of stores were captured, which indicated Rosas hoped to hold the position for a long time. Ouseley thereafter wrote joyfully: "The consequences of this gallant affair, *if we are strong enough to follow it up*, will be very important."[28]

Ouseley's hopes for the overthrow of Rosas were never higher than in December 1845. Paraguay and Corrientes had concluded an alliance, and he had established a friendly, if indefinite, connection with the former as a result of the Parana expedition. In December he learned that Paraguay had sent six to eight thousand men to aid General Paz in Corrientes, and about the same time the Bolivian minister visited Ouseley with another offer. ". . . [if] I could assure him," Ouseley reported privately to Aberdeen, "that our Govt. would not back out & make terms with Rosas—but declare war against this 'great Cause of all the Evils of these countries'—if we could *even verbally*, Bolivia was ready to march 2,000 men against him."[29] Then a few weeks later he wrote again: ". . . if we frankly give a helping hand to Genl. Paz &

Paraguay, we overthrow Rosas in 2 months. I implore Yr. Ldp. not to lose sight that we must strike hard, & at his heart, or Rosas will take fearful vengeance."[30]

In Ouseley's mind was the brilliant vision of a grand alliance of powers in that area of the world, an alliance which, with British advice and some assistance, would go on to create a new order in the La Plata region. All of the opposition movements to the dictator had taken new heart. There was only one factor that Ouseley seemed to overlook. He had been sent to praise Rosas, not to bury him.

———————

Meanwhile back in England, Aberdeen had been harassed by Parliament during the 1845 session on the subject of La Plata. In reply to a question in the Commons in February, Peel revealed that Britain and France, with the concurrence of Brazil, hoped to mediate in the La Plata.[31] In March and April the subject was again mooted in the Lower House. In June questions were put in the Upper House on La Plata affairs on behalf of certain bankers, merchants, and traders of Liverpool; and Aberdeen answered them.[32]

The merchants most interested in the commerce of Uruguay (for those connected with Buenos Aires were strangely silent at this time) seem to have been centered in Liverpool. "The Liverpool Papers are angry and abusive about the state of affairs in the River Plate," Aberdeen wrote Peel in September.[33] Several days later he reviewed the situation for Peel, and apparently showed the Prime Minister Ouseley's instructions for the first time:[34]

Our Ministers have probably fixed some day to receive his [Rosas'] definite answer to their proposition, and this is the cause of the delay & their apparent inactivity. I cannot doubt that Rosas will reject our proposals, & that we shall be under the necessity of having recourse to the measures pointed out in my dispatch. I believe there is no danger of the Baron Deffaudis being disinclined to adopt a vigorous course, but quite the contrary.

Aberdeen's worry at this time was that Ouseley might not proceed fast and vigorously enough!

The defection of a prominent supporter of Rosas' Government, reported to Aberdeen, gave him some hope that coercion might be avoided, but on October 8, 1845 he wrote Ouseley a private letter he was later to regret:[35]

> Although your last dispatches do not actually announce the entire failure of your negotiations with Rosas, there is little room to hope for a favourable change, and I therefore regard coercive measures as having now become indispensable. You have been much censured in this country for the delay which has taken place, but it seems to me that you have acted with moderation and prudence. . . . I confess that I think we are indebted to the Baron Deffaudis for his opposition to your idea of leaving Oribe, under any circumstances, as President of Uruguay, and I am very glad you did not press this further. . . . If measures of coercion have become necessary . . . I trust they will have been executed with vigour, & that we shall not incur the inconvenience & loss of a long blockade. . . . My only ground for uneasiness arises from the possibility of some outrage being committed against the persons or property of British Subjects.

This letter was quite warlike in places, and, as it did not arrive at Montevideo until January, Ouseley saw in it a justification for his moves to depose Rosas. In it Aberdeen also mentioned the opening of the Parana, but he seemed to think this would occur automatically once Martin Garcia were seized. Aberdeen also hoped that spontaneous uprisings would aid the coercion, and thus was guilty of much wishful thinking.

Meanwhile Rosas' effective propaganda campaign in foreign countries began to affect British opinion in commercial circles. "I see his usual clever & indefatigable use of the Press in England, France, Germany, Rio, everywhere," Ouseley wrote in January 1846, "misleading public opinion, creating a general feeling against us, and I find we have no means of replying or counteracting the impression."[36] During the ensuing months Ouseley found evidence of Rosas' propaganda everywhere, not excluding the dispatches sent by Aberdeen and Guizot.[37]

This propaganda campaign in Britain created an entirely different condition of public opinion in late autumn than had existed in the spring. It called to life the active protests of the British interests connected with Argentina, and Aberdeen found himself again attacked by commercial interests, but this time for a different, or rather opposite, reason.

Other factors likewise caused Aberdeen to lose interest in the intervention. Early in November the Corn Law question arose to produce an imminent threat of a Cabinet split. Aberdeen sided with Peel, but the continued existence of the Peel Government was questionable from that time on.[38] Knowing that the Government was living on borrowed time, Aberdeen was anxious to liquidate successfully as many problems as he could.

On November 5, Aberdeen sent new instructions to Ouseley, which prescribed a "more conciliatory course." In a private letter of December 3, he explained his changed position:[39]

> The fact is, that we have been a good deal misled with respect to the nature of this contest, and the condition of the two parties. The agents of Monte Video have been indefatigable and have greatly exaggerated the importance of our interests in that place; while the merchants of Buenos Ayres have been quiescent. It now turns out that the real injury inflicted by the Blockade will be upon English interests and that in fact our fellow countrymen will be the chief sufferers. . . . Finding . . . that the expulsion of Oribe from the Banda Oriental will be extremely difficult . . . it will be a most desirable object to terminate the present state of affairs by promoting, rather than impeding, his settlement in the Town. . . . I wish you would open a confidential communication with Oribe by means of one of his friends in the Town.

This new instruction was, of course, a complete change from his position of October 8, when Oribe was not to be considered for the presidency. It ignored all of the difficulties that such a switch would entail for Ouseley, and also the fact that Oribe was merely the tool of Rosas and would do nothing on his own.

Sir Thomas Paxley arrived in London from the La Plata region later in December, and his account deepened Aberdeen's gloom over Anglo-French prospects. He reported the situation to Peel, who at this time was almost wholly absorbed by the Corn Law situation:[40]

You may perhaps recollect my great reluctance to engage actively in the affairs of the River Plate, and how long I resisted all the Representations upon the Subject made both by the Merchants and in Parliament. I now regret I had not been more obstinate, for we have entered upon a task which it will be scarcely possible for us fully to accomplish, and from which it will not be easy to withdraw with honour. The fact is that we have been greatly misinformed by all the officers professing to have local knowledge, as well as by those more directly interested, with respect to the effect of a naval demonstration, and a blockade. It is now clear that without Troops nothing effectual can be done. Naval operations alone will be very tedious & very uncertain, inflicting at the same time great injury upon our own Merchants, and upon English Commerce.

It was a humiliating situation, but even then not all of the bad news had arrived.

Aberdeen had been impressed before by Ouseley's moderation, and this increased his disappointment when his minister's private letters began to come in. When he learned that the expedition up the Parana was contemplated, Aberdeen wrote: "Is this quite consistent with your instructions? It is not easy to see in what this proceeding differs from actual war."[41] At the same time, he noted: "I wish you clearly to understand that I not only object to your proposal of declaring war on Rosas, but also that you are not to *make war* against Him."

Early in January 1846, Aberdeen learned of the Parana expedition. He made no comment on it immediately. Rather ironically his wish to see France and Britain actively cooperate had at last been granted, but under what circumstances! Many of the developments pleased him, for it was obvious that Franco-British relations were unusually good. But he had the helpless feeling of sinking deeper and deeper into a quagmire without being able to do anything about it.

Unfortunately for both Aberdeen and Ouseley, Parliament again became interested in the situation early in 1846. Guizot saw fit to lay his instructions to Deffaudis before the French legislature, and Aberdeen was unable to resist a demand that he do likewise. Between instructions and events there were a number of discrepancies, and an embarrassing debate took place in the Lords the middle of February. On March 4 Aberdeen wrote Ouseley that the result of the investigation had been to "place Rosas in the eyes of the public as a person who had been treated with violence and injustice." He noted frankly that he had been unable to defend the Parana expedition—"The first shot fired was a great mistake."[42] But he assured Ouseley that he did not propose to write him officially in this manner.

Meanwhile the long delay in communications created a situation which operated to Ouseley's disadvantage. He had received Aberdeen's instruction to open communications with Oribe, but he also heard news that the Peel Government had fallen, as indeed it did momentarily in December. So when he replied to Aberdeen on January 31, Ouseley gave no indication of following the new instructions, but wrote as he would to a private friend, once again advising that "brute force" be applied to remove Rosas. Aberdeen evidently was greatly annoyed that more precious time was being lost while his subordinate argued the case with him. "It is marvellous," he replied, "that you still continue to talk of the necessity of declaring war against Rosas . . . if I had twenty thousand Troops to spare, I would not send one of them."[43]

The Government, which was then encountering many other difficulties, could, of course, solve this one by blaming the whole affair on Ouseley. Peel favored this solution:[44]

I see no alternative but the immediate recall of Ouseley on the express ground of his having exceeded or rather disobeyed his Instructions, and having withheld any sufficient vindication of his conduct for so doing. Mild rebukes, retaining him in his present capacity, would be inconsistent with the Concessions (call them by what name you will) that England and France need make to General Rosas.

Aberdeen, who realized that his own change of policy and the difficulties of communications had contributed to Ouseley's problems, replied that the intervention was popular in France, and that it would be scarcely right to recall Ouseley if Deffaudis remained. "When matters are settled," he added, "we must find some other post for Ouseley, and after what has happened, not leave him accredited to Rosas."[45] Aberdeen, however, felt compelled to write his Dispatch Number 30, wherein, contrary to his assurance to Ouseley of March 4, he censured his subordinate for violating his instructions.

Thereafter Aberdeen decided to send Thomas Hood, an individual known to be friendly both to Rosas and Oribe, on a special mission to see whether he could secure a pacification of the La Plata. In so doing he worked out a new set of instructions with the approval of Guizot, which furnished Hood with wide powers to appease the dictator. On one point Aberdeen neglected to secure a meeting of minds — as to when the blockade should be lifted.

Having made this last effort to achieve peace, Aberdeen was done with the La Plata. His last letter to Ouseley brings forth clearly the issues between the two men:[46]

It is useless to discuss further at present the affairs of the River Plate. We look at them from a point of view essentially different. Your great object is to overthrow Rosas. I should deeply regret this & would not effect it if I could. This fundamental difference necessarily pervaded the character of your whole policy and conduct. We have no complaint whatever in my opinion to make against Rosas, except his reluctance to make peace with Mte. Video. I look upon his lamentations about the American system as mere stuff, not supported by the facts of the case. Commerce appears to be with him perfectly free, and even the access of British goods into the internal waters, in Buenos Ayres vessels, is altogether unopposed. . . . If Rosas should refuse to accept the terms proposed by Guizot & myself, of which Mr. Hood is the bearer, I shall indeed begin to believe that he is as unreasonable as you represent Him to be. . . . On Monday next I believe we are to give up the Seals, after which I shall only be a Spectator of these affairs, but in which it will be impossible not to take a lively interest mingled with some anxiety, until peace shall be actually restored.

Thus, when Aberdeen left office, the outcome of the intervention was still very much in doubt. He was not there when the Hood mission broke down—largely over the question of when the blockade should be lifted.

Aberdeen left Ouseley in a most embarrassing situation

as a result of Dispatch Number 30. In reply the latter wrote a massive sixty-page defense of his conduct.[47] Undoubtedly in organizing the Parana expedition, in recommending war with Rosas, and in siding so completely with Rivera, Ouseley had exceeded the letter of his instructions; whether he violated their "spirit" is another question. His conscientious and stubbornly-held conviction that Rosas must be overthrown, and his slowness, even after receiving instructions, to seek an alternative policy is also a point against him. His private letters to Aberdeen were long, frequently repetitious arguments to sustain his own point of view. If one feels that a minister should act according to his own view of what is best for his country, Ouseley was a very good minister; if one feels he should merely carry out orders from above, then Ouseley does not measure up so well.

Although the events of early 1846 had annoyed him and caused inconvenience to the Government, Aberdeen seems to have appreciated Ouseley's good intentions. In a letter of May 19, he told Ouseley flatly: ". . . I shall be fully disposed to give you another destination as soon as possible."[48] Later on Aberdeen seems to have revised his opinion of Rosas, and to have moved closer to Ouseley's estimation of him. When all was said and done, the best that could be made out of the La Plata venture was that it found British and French sailors as comrades-at-arms in a common, if not a glorious, cause.

## CHAPTER V

# The United States: Knots Untied

WHILE Aberdeen watched helplessly the gradually entangling threads of diplomacy in the La Plata region, he continued during the same period to pick at the tight knots in North America—Texas and Oregon. The former, as we shall see, grew in size to include the problems of California and the Mexican War, and the latter pulled tighter and tighter until it produced a tense, and, to Aberdeen's way of thinking, wholly irrational crisis between the United States and Britain, and almost brought those nations to war.

As we have seen, an equitable compromise of the Oregon question had been accepted by Aberdeen in 1844, though it had not been officially offered to the United States. Also, as was noted above, the United States knew that Aberdeen favored such a compromise, but she took no steps to facilitate its presentation. This writer does not pretend to explain the motives of the American statesmen, but an explanation later offered by Pakenham perhaps deserves some consideration— that the Americans, knowing Aberdeen's pacifism and encouraged to bank on it by Everett, believed a policy of delay would be in their interest, and would eventually bring a complete capitulation by Great Britain.

At any rate, President Polk's policy of looking John Bull "straight in the eye" was perhaps the most effective means that could be employed to prolong the crisis, and to prevent a compromise solution. We know, for instance, that Aberdeen wrote Peel in October 1844: "Its [the Oregon question's] real importance is insignificant, but the Press of both Countries, and publick clamour, have given it a fictitious interest which renders it difficult for either Government to act with moderation, or even common sense. I have no expectation that Mr. Calhoun will agree to any terms that we could venture to propose; but this is no reason for our not exhausting all the means of settlement in our power."[1] As Aberdeen's letter indicates, both countries had become excited over the question, which made a solution difficult. If it is legitimate to blame either the British or American governments for prolonging the crisis, this stigma must rest most heavily on the one which agitated the question most loudly, and thereby stimulated public opinion. In this respect America was probably more guilty than Britain.[2]

The election of James K. Polk, who was committed by his party platform to the extreme 54-40 degree American claim in Oregon, caused Aberdeen once again to offer arbitration. It was declined by Calhoun on January 21, 1845. As the time for Polk's inauguration approached, Sir Robert Peel wrote a long, thoughtful letter to Aberdeen:[3]

The Proceedings of the United States with respect to the Oregon are . . . the most important as immediately affecting the maintenance of amicable relations with the United States. After what has passed in Congress, and after the refusal of arbitration we cannot plead *surprize*—whatever may hereafter take place. These occurrences render compromise and concession (difficult enough before considering what stands on record of past negociations) ten times more difficult now. The point of Honour is now brought into the foreground. What shall we do, in order to be on our guard against infraction or palpable evasion of the Treaty—or some act implying insult and defiance? You seem confident that we have the upper hand on the banks of the Columbia, that the settlers connected with the Hudson's Bay Company are actually stronger than the settlers the subjects of the United States are at present. Have you carefully ascertained this fact? If our subjects are the strongest at this present time— may not their superiority be *speedily* weakened and destroyed by the accession of fresh strength to the Americans? I know the bill for the occupation of the territory has not yet the force of law—but the passing of such a Bill by the h. of r.'s ought to operate as notice to us—and justify precautionary measures. We have as much right under the existing Treaty, I apprehend, to occupy and fortify as the Americans have. It appears to me that an additional frigate at the Mouth of the Columbia, and a small artillery force on shore, would aid most materially the resident British Settlers. What is the most expeditious mode of sending a small artillery force to the Oregon? Probably by sea. Might not a stout frigate be immediately sent from home with sealed orders carrying some marines & artillerymen—professedly for the Cape of Good Hope, or New South Wales, or where you will—but really for the mouth of the Oregon, the destination not being known to anyone but ourselves at the time of sailing?

It will be noted that this pugnacity on the part of the Prime Minister arose in response to events in America, not as a result of opposition attacks. The election slogan of 1844, the refusal of the offer of arbitration, and the debates in the House of Representatives united to cause consternation in Britain. Was this an atmosphere in which Aberdeen could have offered his compromise? Were not the Democrats in the United States making his compromise (which Peel was no doubt alluding to in the above letter) more and more impossible?

As we have seen, Aberdeen opposed war preparations because they contributed to war hysteria. However, at this time his opposition was beginning not only to weaken, but to be engulfed. Roebuck, a Radical, on March 3 told Parliament that Britain was not accustomed to yield to bluster, and asked for papers relating to Oregon. But Peel put him off with the observation that his Government was aware of the importance of the question.[4]

The same day Roebuck made his observations, Aberdeen again directed Pakenham to offer arbitration. The day following, in his inaugural address, Polk raised the "point of Honour" even higher with his famous statement: "Our title to the country of Oregon is 'clear and unquestionable,' and already are our people preparing to perfect that title by occupying it with their wives and children." Aberdeen strove to quiet the storm of indignation which arose as a result of it:[5]

We ought to make all reasonable preparations without delay, but it should be such as may be consistent with the preservation of peace. In spite of Mr. Polk's address, I cannot believe, that when they see us determined, that the American Govt. will drive matters to extremity.

About all that could be done at the moment toward preserving peace was to prevent overt acts by his own Government which might increase the tension.

In a private letter to Pakenham in early April, Aberdeen stressed the growing gravity of the situation. If Britain's offer of arbitration were rejected, and if no counter offer were made by the United States, he did not see how the negotiation could proceed. He continued:[6]

... I presume we must expect that the American Govt. will denounce the Treaty without delay. In this case, unless the question be settled in the course of the year, a local collision must speedily take place, which may too probably involve the Countries in the most serious difficulties, & finally lead to war itself.

At all events ... the time is come when we must endeavour to be prepared for any contingency. Our Naval force in the Pacifick is ample, and Sir George Seymour has been instructed to shew Himself in the neighbourhood of the Columbia. Sir George Simpson, who will deliver this letter to you, has been authorized to take such measures on the part of the Hudson's Bay Company, as may be thought useful & necessary.

... You will hold a temperate, but firm language to the Members of the Govt. & all those with whom you may converse. We are still ready to adhere to the principle of an equitable compromise; but we are perfectly determined to cede nothing to force or menace, and are fully prepared to maintain our Rights. This is the spirit in which Sir. Robt. Peel will answer Lord John Russell the day after tomorrow. ... I have thought it so important that our intentions be clearly known & understood in the United States that I have detained the American Mail, in order that a correct report of Sr. R. Peel's language may arrive at Washington as early as possible.

It is satisfactory to see that there is a good spirit in Parliament & in the Publick & that we shall be supported in whatever course may be really just and necessary.

As appears from its contents, this letter was written in anticipation of a major Opposition attack on the Government policy in Oregon. In the Commons, Peel announced that "we consider we have rights respecting this territory of Oregon which are clear and unquestionable."[7] While Britain would strive for an amicable settlement, she was resolved to maintain her rights. Peel therefore asked that Parliament refrain from complicating the situation further by asking questions regarding it. Although Russell received the explanation in good grace, Palmerston was less satisfied.

In the Lords on the same day, April 4, 1845, Lord Clarendon led off the debate by expressing "surprise and deep regret" at the recent activities of the United States, and asked what England had done to protect her rights. Replying, Aberdeen reviewed the history of the question, then continued as follows:[8]

I am accustomed almost daily to see myself characterized as pusillanimous, cowardly, mean, dastardly, truckling and base. I hope I need not say that I view these appellations with indifference; I view them, indeed, really with satisfaction, because I know perfectly well what they mean, and how they ought to be and are translated. I feel perfectly satisfied that these vituperative terms are to be translated as applicable to conduct consistent with justice, reason, moderation and with common sense; and I therefore feel, as I said before, really not indifference, but positive satisfaction, when I see these observations. I believe I may conscientiously say that no man ever filled the high situation which I have the honour unworthily to hold, who felt more ardently desirous than I do to preserve to the country the blessings of peace, or who would be disposed to make greater sacrifices, consistent with propriety, to maintain it. [cheers] My Lords, I consider war to be the greatest folly, if not the greatest crime, of which a country could be guilty, if lightly entered into; and I agree entirely with a moral writer who has said, that if a proof were wanted of the deep and thorough corruption of human nature, we should find it in the fact that war itself was sometimes justifiable. [cheers] It is the duty, and I am sure it is the inclination of Her Majesty's Government to preserve peace; at the same time there are limits which must not be passed; and I say that, without attaching too much weight to questions of national honour—for I think, fortunately for this country, that we need not be very sensitive in these matters—it is not for us, God knows, to "seek the bubble reputation at the cannon's mouth," or anywhere else; our power, our character and position, are such as to enable us to look with indifference on that of which other countries might be, perhaps, jealous. [cheers] But our honour is a substantial property that we can certainly never neglect, and most assuredly we may owe it to ourselves and to our posterity to adopt a course contrary to all our desires, to all our inclinations. My Lords, from what I have said, your

Lordships will perceive an earnest of the spirit of peace which shall pervade this matter, if I continue to conduct the negotiation; and I cannot bring myself to think that at this day any civilized Government would desire to see any other course pursued; and I hope, therefore, and fully believe, that we shall have the happiness of seeing this important question brought to a satisfactory because an amicable conclusion. [loud cheers] Should it be otherwise, I can only say that we possess rights which, in our opinion, are clear and unquestionable; and, by the blessing of God, and your support, those rights we are fully prepared to maintain.

Although Aberdeen was not a Stanley or an Ellenborough, this speech evidently was delivered with the eloquence which springs from conviction and high purpose. One authority calls it an "impressive warning" to the United States.[9] That element was certainly present, but present also was a warning to the Opposition not to expect him to uphold an exaggerated sense of national honor. Aberdeen's condemnation of war as an instrument of national policy shows him at his best. All in all, the speech echoed the firm, but conciliatory policy which he was to maintain throughout the remainder of the negotiation.[10]

The effect of the aggressive attitude of the United States is reflected in Aberdeen's private letter to Pakenham shortly after the above speech. Once again he explained that if Buchanan would offer the Everett compromise ". . . I should not like to regard his proposal as inadmissible. It is possible that by some modifications it might be accepted, although I do not think it at all likely, & of course you will give no encouragement to the notion. . . ."[11] In his letter of March 4, 1844, he had said: "I think you might give them reason to hope that such a proposal would be favourably considered." Thus the bluster of the United States had produced a corresponding stiffening of the British attitude.

Though he was in receipt of these instructions, Pakenham shortly was guilty of a major diplomatic blunder. The American Secretary of State, James Buchanan, on July 12, 1845, advised the British minister that the United States was ready to divide the Oregon territory at the 49th parallel. As this offer had been turned down by his Government on three previous occasions, Pakenham rejected it without reference to higher authority. This placed the British Government in an awkward position.

Peel thought Pakenham's rejection was "needlessly harsh and preemptory," and predicted the United States would not relinquish the diplomatic advantage she had gained, but he opposed any further concession as a means of setting things right.[12] Aberdeen, who was assured by the new American minister, Louis McLane, that Polk and Buchanan were distressed at this sudden stoppage of the negotiation, instructed Pakenham to try to secure the withdrawal of the letters which had passed between Buchanan and himself. If this were refused, nothing would be lost, for "no record will exist of our overture."[13] He wrote Pakenham, ". . . very much depends upon the real feelings of the President and Mr. Buchanan."[14]

By this time Peel seems to have lost all confidence in the United States. He wrote Aberdeen:[15]

It is *because* I think the Government of the United States is dishonest, because I believe they are trying to find pretexts for delay or evasion, I would have put Mr. Buchanan in the difficulty in which he would have been put by not peremptorily rejecting his proposal.

It was a gloomy autumn indeed. The Oregon negotiations seemed to have reached a deadlock, and a useless and expensive war might yet result over a sterile question of national honor.

Meanwhile the election of Polk, for which Aberdeen should have been prepared[16] and which had done so much to complicate the Oregon question, likewise had its influence on the problem of Texas. The Cabinet felt that Polk's election was compensated for to some extent by the election of Anson Jones, generally thought to favor an independent Texas, as president of that republic. Jones was inaugurated in December 1844, the same month that Santa Anna was overthrown and replaced in Mexico by Jose Herrera.

Santa Anna's fall caused some diplomatic confusion similar to that which obtained in early 1843. Aberdeen had finally agreed to recognize an independent Texas with a Colorado

River boundary, and he advised the Texan charge, George W. Terrell, of this fact on January 20, 1845. Aberdeen stated further that he was aware this boundary was unacceptable to Texas, but he said Britain and France would cooperate to establish Texan independence once it was granted. He emphasized, however, the use of "moral force" rather than going to "extremity." Dispatches were sent to Elliot on the subject, but all this preparation was in vain.

Santa Anna, of course, had already fallen at the time Aberdeen spoke with Terrell, and the dispatches were, therefore, valueless. The initiative for the last serious British intervention into Texan affairs came, in fact, from President Anson Jones, and not from Aberdeen. When he learned that the American House of Representatives had passed the annexation resolution on January 25, 1845, Jones wrote to Elliot as follows:[17]

> The resolution on the subject of annexation passed by the U.S. Representatives is quite unsatisfactory to our people so far as I have heard any opinion expressed, and I am more than ever of the mind that they would prefer Independence and peace to any other measure. From what I learned from Navarro and from other sources it would appear that the new Government of Mexico are favorably disposed to an amicable settlement of matters, and I have taken some measures to invite their attention to the subject. Could a fair proposition be made and reach us by the middle of May or even the 1st June with a suitable endorsement I think it would be well. I may be mistaken about the action of others, but for myself I should have no doubt of the course in that case to be pursued.

Elliot was doubtful that the Texans really wanted independence.[18] Both Aberdeen and Peel had likewise lost their enthusiasm for projects in this area of the world, and the latter was wholly out of touch with the situation.[19] To Aberdeen the situation afforded at most another opportunity to cooperate with France, but the time was short, London was far from the scene, and he actually had little part in Elliot's project.

Elliot and the French minister, Alphonso de Saligny, using their own discretion and the instructions on hand, had a

conference with Ashbel Smith and Anson Jones during
March 27-29, 1845. They were promised that Texas would
not negotiate for annexation to the United States for a period
of 90 days, and during that time the mediators might seek
to secure Mexican recognition of Texan independence. They
also agreed that Texas, under these circumstances, would
remain independent. So the first episode, to Elliot's way of
thinking, went off well.[20]

Acting on his own initiative, Elliot assured Anson Jones
that he would go secretly to Mexico and do what he could
to prod the Mexican legislature into action. Later he wrote
Aberdeen:[21]

It is to be regretted that the Mexican Government have not
been able to complete this transaction for so considerable a
period of time, for it may be taken for granted that the American
Government and Agents have sedulously availed themselves of
the interval to indispose the people of Texas against adjustment upon this footing.

As the Mexican Government stalled, Anson Jones, yielding
to popular pressure, called a session of the Texan Congress
for June 16 to consider the annexation offer from the United
States. But in so doing he did not break his promise to Elliot
regarding the time limit during which he would receive a
Mexican offer.

Back in London Aberdeen was passive. Early in April
he wrote Pakenham that the subject of Texas was "so difficult
& complicated & is characterized by so much that is new
& unprecedented that it will require much consideration before we can finally shape our course."[22] Late in May, when
it seemed Britain might actually be called upon to arbitrate
a boundary between Texas and Mexico, he wrote Bankhead
they would ignore the "extravagant pretensions" on both
sides in reaching a settlement.[23] In a later letter Aberdeen
told Bankhead to warn Mexico that her failure to recognize
Texas would result in Britain and France washing their
hands of further responsibility for the future.

The news of Elliot's activities was received with mixed
feelings by Sir Robert Peel:[24]

Captain Elliot appears not only to have acted with the best of intentions, but probably to have taken the best course which it was open to him to take. Should the Congress refuse to ratify the act of the Texian Executive and shd. Captain Elliot's secret mission be discovered, our failure to prevent annexation will be more marked and give more triumph to the United States than if Captain Elliot had been less active and had less of temporary success. Be this however as it may. He deserves credit for his conduct in every respect except the Journey to Mexico.

Peel realized immediately that Elliot's secret mission would be interpreted as an underhanded bit of diplomatic activity scarcely creditable to a great nation, and he was not wrong in this anticipation.

In London Terrell, even at this late date, gave the strong impression to Aberdeen that he opposed annexation. As he was about to return to Texas early in June 1845, he asked Aberdeen about the status of Mexican recognition of Texas. He added:[25]

. . . if I am enabled to say to the people of Texas that I know the fact that the Mexican Govt. are prepared to acknowledge our independence if we will reject the propositions of the U. States for Annexation, I believe it will have a great deal of weight with them in determining this great question. . . . The Congress . . . can do nothing more than signify their approbation of the measure, and provide for the calling of a Convention of the people through delegates chosen for the purpose—so that the great battle will be fought before the people at last, and this will require some months, and I wish to be there, and armed as strongly as possible for the contest.

But Aberdeen could give him no such assurance, only a "confident hope" that Mexico would recognize Texas. "I think it right to add," he observed significantly, "that the reluctance evinced by the Mexican Govt. in coming to this decision, was chiefly owing to an apprehension that the independence of Texas, when acknowledged, would not necessarily be preserved inviolate."[26]

Events moved quickly in the New World. Elliot presented the Mexican offer to Anson Jones on June 4, and he proclaimed peace with Mexico. The Texan Congress, however, snubbed the Mexican offer, and at its meeting between

June 16-28 unanimously approved annexation to the United States. Thereupon Jones set the date for the Convention for July 4. In spite of Terrell's prediction, the acceptance of the American offer by the Convention was immediate. Thereafter some details such as the adoption of a state constitution had to be worked out, but on February 19, 1846 Texas formally became part of the United States.

Insofar as Britain was concerned, a new phase had been reached. And it was one Aberdeen had foreseen and dreaded for some time.

———————

In spite of the close collaboration between France and Britain in the La Plata and Texas incidents, Aberdeen had been unable to convince the rest of the Cabinet—Wellington and Peel, at any rate—of the soundness of the Anglo-French entente. Peel continued to be suspicious of France in Greece and North Africa, while Wellington was convinced that the traditional French hatred of England could not be overcome. Between the two countries the question of the Spanish marriages likewise tended to create suspicion.[27]

As a result of the differences with the United States over Oregon, Wellington once again began to press forward his preparedness program. Canada continued to be a problem, for the Cabinet was not quite sure that this province wanted to be defended in case of war with the United States. The Governor General there evidently recommended a preventive war against the United States in the autumn of 1845, but the Cabinet saw fit to conceal this recommendation from the Duke.

Aberdeen by this time was less opposed than before to precautions against a possible war with the United States. But it was the other aspect of the Duke's program which bothered him. In September Peel wrote:[28]

I presume Guizot is aware that our relations with the United States are uneasy, and that he cannot be surprised after the proceedings adopted and the doctrines avowed with regard to Texas and the American Continent if we are on the alert in Canada and our other North American Provinces.

In his reply Aberdeen tended to ignore the American question, and instead complained that a serious difference of opinion had developed between Peel and Graham and himself on French policy. While admitting there was always a possibility of going to war with France, he called the present efforts of the Duke for preparedness "childish restlessness." He wrote:[29]

A policy of friendship and confidence has been converted into a policy of hostility and distrust. . . . I cannot too strongly express my dissent from the spirit and motives by which they will have been suggested. It is my deliberate and firm conviction that there is less reason to distrust the French Government at the present moment, than there was four years ago, when administration was first formed. . . . Under all the circumstances to which I have referred, and the apprehensions I entertain, it is my belief that it will be the safest course for you to allow me to retire from the Government. . . .

Peel replied that he had "insuperable objections" to Aberdeen's resignation, and that he would consider the loss "irreparable."

It was at this point that the offer of California was made by Mexico, an offer which must have been rather tempting because it afforded another opportunity to strengthen the Anglo-French entente. Some background information, however, is necessary if this offer is to be considered in its proper setting.

With the failure of the Diplomatic Act, Lord Aberdeen decided upon a policy of non-interference in affairs between the United States and Mexico. On October 23, 1844 he wrote Bankhead in Mexico to advise that Government that he regretted the failure of the Diplomatic Act, and that he still viewed "the annexation of Texas to the United States as an evil of the greatest magnitude to Mexico."[30] He clarified Britain's position further in a dispatch of December 31, 1844. Pointing to the need of the buffer state of Texas between the United States and Mexico, Aberdeen observed: ". . . when once that nation [the United States] shall have obtained possession of Texas; from that moment H. M. Govt. wd. consider the existence of the Republic of Mexico as seriously threatened. You will also clearly explain to the Mexican Govt. that they must not count upon the assistance of Great Britain, whose friendly advices they have always constantly neglected."[31]

Aberdeen did not consider the Elliot mission as a breach of the non-interference policy, for Britain promised no more than to use her moral influence to bring the countries together. The most he promised in his dispatch of May 31, 1845 was that Britain would not view "with indifference" the violation of the frontier which might be established between Texas and Mexico as a result of her mediation.[32] So, despite the obviously growing danger to Mexico, Aberdeen chose to disentangle his country from the politics of the Rio Grande region.

He knew full well that the British withdrawal might result in complete disaster to Mexico. Bankhead, who was a much more capable observer than Pakenham, reported in July 1845:[33]

It is quite clear, that as far as Mexico is concerned, Texas is lost. To satisfy National Honour (however incapable she may be to sustain it) Mexico thinks it necessary to send an Army to Texas. That Army will dwindle to nothing, and . . . the State of Affairs between the United States & Mexico will stand exactly where they were, and the war may eventually end by some humiliating peace. . . . New Mexico and Coahuila will become a Second Texas. To avoid this, it appears to me . . . it would be advisable, if possible, to bring the contending Parties to some mutual & honourable understanding.

About this time Bankhead offered to pay Mexico a sum of money to secure the exclusive territorial and commercial rights over California. This, however, was a private offer, and in no way involved the British Government.[34]

Thus it appeared that war between the United States and Mexico was not improbable, and that such a war would result in further losses of territory for Mexico. On September 23, therefore, the Mexican minister in London visited Aberdeen, who reported the interview as follows:[35]

The Mexican Minister came to me today, & said that war was certain with the U. States, & that he had no doubt they would be able to stand their ground on the Texan frontier; but that the distance of California was so great, and the country so thinly inhabited, & the resources of the Government so much impoverished that it would be impossible to defend the Province . . . Under these circumstances He was entrusted to propose to me some arrangement by which it should be to our interest to protect California from the Invasion of the U. States. He had no specific proposal to make, but the Govt. would be ready to agree to any terms which should have the effect of excluding the U. States. . . . I told the Mexican Minister that I would give him no answer. He must be perfectly aware of our desire to keep the U. States out of California if possible; but that I could not say in what manner we could contribute to this end. I told him that even if we could allow such an English interest to be constituted in California as would give us a right to protect the Province, this could not be done without exciting the jealousy of other Powers; and that in whatever it might be possible to do, I wished to act in concert with France.

After this interview Aberdeen contacted the French minister on the subject, and said that he was "inclined" to concert with France on the subject. ". . . if we could succeed in enlisting France," Aberdeen continued, "for their own interest, cordially tọ unite in resisting American aggression, it would be a great stroke öf policy, & go far to change the whole face of affairs. They began well, but timidly, in Texas; perhaps a direct interest may make them bolder in California." At the same time Aberdeen predicted that the French would not adopt any effective course.

Peel was somewhat embarrassed at the timing of this offer, for it was made just at the moment Wellington was pressing for warlike preparations against France, and Aberdeen was obviously using it as a means of forestalling such preparations. He replied:[36]

The Mexican offer as to California comes I fear too late. Even if there were no other objection to the acceptance of it, I doubt whether it would not be better to declare boldly and frankly that on considerations of general policy we would resist the conquest of California by the United States, than after the declaration of war on the part of Mexico, or on the Eve of its Declaration, to attempt to establish such an English interest. . . .

If the interest had bona fide existed at the commencement of hostilities, the character of our intervention would be different. But the hasty establishment of it under present circumstances would have a suspicious appearance, and would give a selfish character to our interference.

Peel expressed doubts that any English capitalist would make such an investment in California without special guarantees. Then he concluded stiffly: "It appears to me that you have acted wisely in attempting to ascertain in the first instance and without delay whether France is disposed Cordially to unite with us in preventing the Conquest and annexation of California by the United States."

In his reply to Peel, Aberdeen quietly pointed out the defect in the Prime Minister's reasoning with regard to "considerations of general policy": [37]

War has not yet been declared by Mexico, and they would no doubt if necessary regulate their mode of proceeding in this respect so as to render our course more easy. The question seems now to be tolerably simple. I am clearly of opinion that we ought not to interfere singly. If England and France should think proper, from notions of general policy, to declare that they will not suffer California to be invaded, this is war against the United States; for no independent Power would tolerate such a limitation being imposed upon their free action, without war. There is not the least chance of France being prepared to take any such course. It is barely possible that if an English and French interest were created in the Province sufficient to justify our interfering, this might take place without leading to war, and it is also possible that this might offer a sufficient temptation to France to act with us. But I do not expect that anything can come of this suggestion; in which case, we have no alternative but to leave the field open to the U. States.

It is clear that Aberdeen was already certain that major territorial adjustments would result from an American conflict with Mexico. This prospect does not seem to have disturbed him deeply.

Early in October the French reply was received, and Aberdeen reported Guizot's reaction in a letter to Peel.[38]

The Subject of California was more favourably received than I expected although as I had made no specifick suggestion he could give no positive opinion. But he repeated that he was determined to act with us in America whenever it was possible, and that he would persevere in abandoning the old French policy of connection with the U. States. He had done this in Texas, in spite of much opposition, and would not hesitate to do so again when any opportunity should occur. He wished to have some intelligible proposal of the course we desired to adopt in California, in order to see whether He could adopt it at once. Notwithstanding these friendly declarations, however, I am by no means of opinion that either Guizot or the King is at all prepared to incur the risk of war with the U. States for the sake of California; nor do I know that we should be justified in pressing them to adopt such a course. I have written strongly to Bankhead in Mexico and have desired him to do everything in his power to prevent war, if there be yet time. The Mexican Minister seems to think that war is inevitable, and speaks with great confidence of their means of carrying it on successfully. But California, of which all the towns are situated on the coast of the Pacifick, and which are at such an immense distance from the Metropolis, must necessarily fall before the first Naval force which appears against them.

This is the last of the private letters regarding California, but it is not difficult to ascertain why the project did not prosper.

Perhaps the most important part of the above letter is the second sentence. Guizot apparently gave Aberdeen the impression that he, too, was consciously trying to break the Franco-American connection. A second point of interest is the complete subordination of economic considerations, which are merely incidental, to those of a diplomatic nature. A third point is Aberdeen's attitude toward bringing France to the brink of war with the United States. While this would have served his policy admirably, he does not feel justified at this time in taking such a step.

This letter also helps clarify Aberdeen's policy toward the Mexican War. In a dispatch of October 1, he urged Bankhead to endeavor to prevent war between the United States and Mexico, and told him to warn the Mexican Government that Britain would do no more than submit "sound and useful suggestions."[39] This was a mild and useful policy,

which followed the advice of Bankhead himself in his private
letter of July 30, 1845.

Peel, however, opposed the mediation scheme, or at least
that part of it which might actually result in a peaceful
solution of the difficulties between the United States and
Mexico. He wrote on November 14:[40]

> It may be quite becoming to Mr. Bankhead's selection to give
> advice to Mexico—seeing how little are the prospects of success—
> to forebear from going to war, but his intervention in making
> an arrangement between Mexico and the United States appears
> to me to involve very difficult considerations. An arrangement
> between Mexico and the United States—sanctioning the annexa-
> tion of Texas by the latter, promoted by the British Minister
> includes us nearly as much as it includes Mexico. It commits
> us to the principle of annexation, makes us acquiescing parties
> in the deed, implies that we have no ground of Complaint against
> either party in the annexation—the United States or Texas.
> Now it is one thing to remain passive, to forebear from
> considerations of policy to urge even an unquestionable Right,
> and another to be parties to an arrangement and to the promotion
> of an arrangement between Mexico and the United States, the
> Basis of which I apprehend must be the fulfillment of the scheme
> of annexation.

Just what Peel hoped to gain by maintaining an air of passive
disapproval of an annexation which was obviously a fact, is
open to question. This attitude has a sulky quality about it
scarcely of credit to this outstanding statesman, but his
views formed the basis of Aberdeen's dispatch of November
28, 1845.

Peel's attitude can, perhaps, he explained in part by his
continuing controversy with Aberdeen regarding the preparedness policy. As we have noted above, this policy caused
the Foreign Minister to offer his resignation in September
1845—a resignation which Peel could not possibly accept
without doing irreparable harm to his Government. So it
was rejected, but the debate continued.

In October Aberdeen wrote the Prime Minister:[41]

> I am glad to perceive that Guizot agrees with me in the
> opinion which I have long entertained & have frequently ex-

pressed, that the old maxim of *preparing for war in order to preserve peace,* is entirely inapplicable to the condition of Great Powers, & to the political System of modern times, and present state of society.

To this Peel sent a rejoinder:[42]

I am a strenuous advocate for Peace—for Peace with France especially, for a friendly understanding with France, for the exhibition by the Ministers of the two countries of forebearance, of an earnest wish to control the senseless cry for War of vile newspapers, and to prevent causes of misunderstanding by conciliatory conduct and honourable compromises. But when I see the weakness of Civil authority in France—the fruitful germs of War with France which will spring up in the event of War with the United States—when I look back at the suddenness with which there have been within our short memories revolutions in the Govt. of France and look forward to the events which *may* occur on the death of L. Philippe, I cannot feel sanguine as to the future.

This letter once again illustrates the extent to which the Franco-American connection preyed on the minds of British statesmen.

In reply Aberdeen called the preparedness program mere "panic," and he retorted feelingly:[43]

Our policy is now changed; and every newspaper is filled with the accounts of our hostile preparations. We still talk of peace, having war in our hearts. I confess that I regret this recent and great change, for which I see no good reason; and I regret it the more, and indeed chiefly, because it is but too probable that it may lead to the very consequences we most desire to avoid.

Thereafter Aberdeen seized with almost pathetic eagerness upon every small incident in an attempt to prove his point. Late in October he talked with the French Opposition leader, Adolphe Thiers, who assured him that he approved Guizot's policy of friendship with England, and that the only "war party" in France was composed of a "few Carlists" on the right and some Radicals and Bonapartists on the left.[44] In November he wrote Peel that the British minister in Mexico was mediating a dispute between the

French minister there and the Mexican Government, which affords "some proof of the existence of the *entente!*"[45] Peel's reply was filled with sarcasm:[46]

It will be a good example to set for the avoidance of quarrels public and private for two Countries having a frivolous dispute on a point of Honour instead of fighting a duel to choose an umpire and abide by his award. The anti-dueling Society will greatly applaud this act.

Of considerably more importance to an understanding of Anglo-American relations was another of Aberdeen's letters, one written after the Presidential Message of December 1845:[47]

You will have observed in the President's message a passage which must be very offensive to France & which I see the French Papers are already beginning to notice. This reference to France in the Message will produce exactly the effect we most desire, and will greatly promote the policy, which I hope may be considered as successful—the separation of France in feeling & interest from the United States.

By this time Peel's mind had been turned to domestic affairs, and no letter is available which states his opinion of the success of Aberdeen's project.

While this argument continued, Aberdeen meanwhile watched the events in Mexico as a passive spectator. The reports he received were, to say the least, conflicting. Pakenham wrote:[48]

It seems to me that the Americans greatly underrate the difficulties and expense of a war with Mexico. Unless the Mexican character has undergone a great change since I left that country, I think the Americans will meet if not with a gallant resistance, at least a sullen and dogged resolution to protract the struggle to the utmost. . . .

On the other hand, Bankhead reported: "At this moment, My Lord, Mexico may be said to be without an Army—at least one in the slightest degree to be depended on. . . . Nothing, My Lord, I am convinced can save this Country from Anarchy & the fatal grasp of the United States but a Monarchy."[49] He suggested that England, France, and Spain unite to set up a monarchy in Mexico while there was still something to save. Fifteen years later his suggestion was to some extent acted upon.

When war broke out between the United States and Mexico in 1846, the latter appealed to England for support. In his "Answer to the Mexican Govt. Requesting Support in their Contest with the United States," Aberdeen recorded the official position of his nation with regard to the Mexican War:[50]

In Nos. 16, 30, 34, 49 and 53 (1844) the intentions and senti- ments of H. M. Govt. were fully and clearly made known. These sentiments and intentions remain unchanged. The recent events wh. have occurred in Mexico are far from affording H. M. Govt. any reasonable ground for departing from the line of policy, wh. in 1844 they found it expedient to adopt. On the contrary they see in those events more & more cause for rigidly adhering to the system of *non*-interference wh. they had pre- scribed for themselves. . . . Mexico, although menaced, and now indeed, as we learn, actually engaged in hostilities on her Texian frontier . . . at the very moment when unity and concord were most necessary to guide the country through the perils wh. beset it, the Govt. was once more subverted by a military revolution. . . .

It is moreover obvious that were Great Britain to interfere in that quarrel she would involve herself in a war with the United States, and not only that, but she must necessarily play the part, not merely of an auxiliary, but of a principal in such a war. That is, she would find herself engaged in a war with a nation with which she has no personal cause to quarrel in behalf of a nation and Govt. she has repeatedly warned . . . of their danger, and which solely in consequence of their wilful contempt of that warning at last plunged headlong down the precipice from wh. the British Govt. spared no efforts to save them.

While Bankhead was allowed to make a "friendly interposi- tion" to save Mexico he could go no further than that. This whole dispatch expresses a complete lack of confidence or trust in the Mexican Government.

This dispatch provided the period to the lengthy para- graphs of British intervention in the affairs of Texas and Mexico. Complex and novel in so many of its aspects, fraught alike with impressive opportunities and real dangers, the situation was the most involved of all that Aberdeen had to face in the New World, and had drawn from him his boldest stroke of diplomacy. Aberdeen felt no twinge of regret at closing the book, even though he was well aware that Brother Jonathan, who was growing prodigiously, would not fail to make the most of his opportunities.

––––––––––

As we have seen, the autumn of 1845 was a most difficult period for Aberdeen. The controversy with Peel and Wellington over rearmament, the imminence of Mexico's war with the United States, the strange turn of affairs in the La Plata region, and, beginning in November, the Corn Law crisis— these momentous events filled to the brim his portmanteau of problems. It is not strange that he forewent his annual visit to Scotland that year.

Late in the summer some good news had finally arrived from America when Robert B. Rhett of South Carolina visited Aberdeen. Aberdeen reported to Peel:[51]

He is the man who proposed the vote of *nullification*, & will do so again if necessary. He is confident that the Tariff will be greatly modified, & is prepared to lead the attack, to which he says that Mr. Polk himself is friendly. But he complains that this Rough Rice question meets them at every step, and paralyzes their efforts. . . .

Anglo-American trade relations, then, seemed on the brink of improvement.

The "Rough Rice" question arose when Britain, contrary to the convention of 1815, had laid certain duties on rough rice, which resulted in an American claim for reimbursement of the excess charges. It had been a perennial thorn, embarrassing rather than virulent, in Aberdeen's side, and had caused a protracted controversy with his friend, Everett. It was the more embarrassing because Aberdeen was convinced Britain was wrong. This was admitted in a letter to Peel, which also provided the solution to the problem:[52]

. . . I have felt quite ashamed to continue the discussion in direct opposition to the provisions of the Treaty, & the explicit declaration of opinion by the three law officers. We have recently made a claim upon the United States of considerably greater amount, which although not quite so clear as theirs, is founded upon the same article of the Treaty. The American Govt. have declined to agree to this claim, as Everett told me, by his advice.

Being anxious to settle the matter before the meeting of Congress Aberdeen prepared a dispatch in which he proposed that the two countries recognize each other's claims. He sent this dispatch to Peel on September 17, 1845, and it led to an amicable settlement of the problem.[53]

But the major issue between Britain and the United States—the Oregon question—remained as a ragged, open wound, daily becoming more inflamed. Late that autumn the prospect of the presidential message caused considerable nervousness among the British leaders. In November Aberdeen wrote Peel:[54]

A Second Edition of the Mg. Herald today had published an extract from a Washington Paper, which it is said, and I believe truly, to speak the language of the President. Should this really be the case & the paragraph in question gives us an accurate notion of the President's message, we must prepare for serious consequences!

Edward Everett's communications, however, tended to allay Aberdeen's fears. This is obvious from one of Peel's letters of early December:[55]

If Mr. Everett assures you that the Whig Party in the United States would agree to arbitration on the Oregon Question, I think considering the opinions expressed by Mr. Calhoun, even Polk dare not resort to extreme measures.

His communications with Everett and Louis McLane, his successor in London, led Aberdeen to expect a strong declaration from Polk, but erased his fear of it. For this reason, he wrote Pakenham:[56]

Notwithstanding the unpromising appearance of the present state of the negociation, I feel satisfied that we are now nearer a settlement than ever. If we press arbitration, they must either accept it, or give us facilities for reopening the direct negociation. If they do neither, they will be so manifestly in the wrong, that

I greatly doubt their receiving the necessary support, even from the hostile portion of the American Publick. I expect a strong declaration from the President in his annual message & even a recommendation to terminate the Treaty. I shall not at all regret this; for as the crisis becomes more imminent, the chance of settlement improves.

Aberdeen evidently believed that an intensification of the crisis would break the deadlock because it would force the American Government to forego its tactics of delay.

Peel and others in the Cabinet, who were not convinced by the advice of Everett and Louis McLane, were alarmed when the text of Polk's message reached Britain. Peel wrote:[57]

I had not time to ask what you thought of the President's message. I advise silence and preparation. I would unite the civil and military Government of Canada in the same hands. I know no one better qualified than Fitzroy Somerset.

In another letter Peel declared: "We shall not reciprocate blustering with Polk, but shall quietly make an increase in Naval and Military and Ordnance Estimates."[58] That active military preparations began to be made at this time is indicated by Ripon's letter to Hardinge in India:[59]

The President's Message to Congress at Washington is threatening in its tone; but it may end in smoke. At the same time we must be upon *our guard and watchful* everywhere. Aden is an important point, and I have called Arthur's attention to it, in respect to both its land fortifications and Naval defense by Steamers.

Ripon promised to send a formal communication on the subject later.

Aberdeen, who believed his offer of arbitration would cause the reopening of negotiations, again sought to restrain his colleagues. To Peel he wrote:[60]

I am glad he has brought matters to an issue, and whether the Senate adopt his recommendation or not, I cannot doubt that we shall see a reasonable settlement. I have never been afraid of the Oregon question, & feel confident that in the course of the year we shall see it finally settled, either by arbitration, or by direct negotiation.

He further advised Peel that Pakenham had received more precise instructions regarding arbitration. Thus Aberdeen hoped the problem would be solved by arbitration, or at least that the offer would cause negotiations to be reopened. Since the United States Senate had not yet accepted the President's recommendation to terminate the joint occupation of Oregon (the debate lasted until April 27, 1846), the time element was not yet too pressing.

Aberdeen meanwhile did what he could to smooth the way for a negotiated settlement.[61] But he could not go beyond the Everett compromise in his concessions. On January 3, 1846 he wrote Everett as follows:[62]

The truth is that everything depends on the real disposition of the President, and of the people by whom he is directed, whether Ministers, or Mob. There is no real difficulty in the matter, and if Mr. McLane had full powers, I think it probable that we would settle it in an hour. We are sincerely and anxiously desirous of a peaceful issue, and if you share this desire, we shall assuredly arrive at it. But if you desire war, as assuredly you will have it, for well as you know my love of peace, and my determination to preserve it, I shall be perfectly powerless in such a case.

Everett, who with the best intentions may well have prolonged the crisis by overemphasizing Aberdeen's conciliatory disposition, in his reply referred to his own compromise discussed before. "I have naturally inferred, though you have never said so," he wrote, "that you would finally agree on that basis," and concluded: "Let us now, for Heaven's sake, take a fresh start."[63] In his anxiety to break the impasse, Everett had even seen fit to ask Lord John Russell, the Opposition leader, to refrain from attacking the Government on this subject.[64]

Both Everett's and McLane's attitudes were very reassuring, but even before Everett wrote the above letter, the United States had taken a step which staggered Aberdeen. Replying in a letter of January 3, 1846 to Pakenham's offer of arbitration of December 28, Buchanan not only rejected the proposal, but made no move to reopen the negotiation. From this Aberdeen could only infer that the United States was purposely prolonging the negotiation, hoping for a concession of the 49th parallel so that the full American object would be achieved.

Aberdeen's response is explained in a letter to Pakenham:[65]

When I received your dispatch enclosing Mr. Buchanan's answer. . . . I told him [McLane] that the reason assigned for the rejection of the proposal . . . was most extraordinary . . . the obstinate refusal of Mr. Buchanan to renew the proposal he had made to you, and which he had since withdrawn, almost led me to doubt the sincerity of the President and Mr. Buchanan in their expressed desire to arrive at a pacifick conclusion of the affair. The difficulty of our present situation, and in our uncertainty respecting the real designs of the American Govt., together with the character of the proceedings of Congress, had made it a matter of prudence to prepare for the worst. I told him . . . it was quite impossible for me to refuse my assent to those measures of preparation which were considered indispensable, both in this country, and in Canada. Mr. McLane protested his conviction that the President and his Govt. were perfectly sincere in their desire to preserve peace. . . . We carried on the discussion for some time in a very friendly manner, but always with a view to the possible failure of our endeavours to preserve peace, at least on my part. . . .

McLane reported the interview to his Government in a dispatch of February 3:[66]

He [Lord Aberdeen] further remarked, that although he would not abandon the desire or the hope that an amicable adjustment might yet be effected, and peace preserved, he should nevertheless feel it his duty to withdraw the opposition he had hitherto uniformly made to the adoption of measures founded upon the contingency of war with the United States, and to offer no obstacle in [the] future to preparations which might be deemed necessary not only for the defense and protection of the Canadas, but for offensive operations. In the course of the conversation, I understood that these would consist independent of military armaments, of the immediate equipment of thirty sail of the line besides steamers and other vessels of war, of a smaller class. . . .

Since these men were good friends, it seems possible that McLane may even have encouraged Aberdeen to make this threat. At any rate, he later sent the portion of his dispatch quoted above to the British Foreign Secretary.

That the British Government feared war might result is evident from one of Lord Ripon's letters to Hardinge, written just after the above:[67]

If the Yankees should force us into an *Oregon* War, Singapore might be tempting bait to some well-armed Privateer, with which I have no doubt they would take care that the seas should swarm. It is in reference to this (*tho' not so stated*) that a Court letter to you goes out asking for the report of Captain Best. . . .

These preparations were no doubt actually defensive, but they were designed to impress the United States regarding Britain's firmness of purpose, and Polk noted them in his speech of March 24, 1846. They were probably the decisive factor in breaking the diplomatic deadlock.[68]

After the final settlement was reached on June 15, 1846, Lord Aberdeen was very warm in his praise of Louis McLane, and it seems probable that the American minister actually laid the groundwork for the compromise. No doubt he gave official assurances to Aberdeen that the Everett compromise would be accepted by the United States and would not become a stepping-stone to demands for further concessions from the British Government. Thus reassured, Aberdeen could send his offer to Pakenham with the observation: "Without calling this Convention an *ultimatum*, it will in fact be so, as far as you are concerned. . . ."[69] McLane also made Aberdeen privy to the scheme by which the American President, in order to preserve his own consistency, passed the convention on to the Senate for action there. In spite of all that has been written on the Oregon question, this final phase merits closer study.[70]

Britain's position, because of American's involvement with Mexico, was at this time very strong. Aberdeen, in fact, wrote Pakenham in May that if some state of affairs had arisen in the United States which in his judgment would justify such action he might suspend the proposals.[71] Pakenham replied that he hoped Aberdeen was not referring to the Mexican War in making this suggestion, for ". . . it would be neither politick nor worthy of a Country like England to make any difference in our manner of dealing with the

Oregon question on account of the existing state of things between Mexico & this Country."[72] Aberdeen replied that he did not have the Mexican War in mind, and that Pakenham was right in not allowing it to influence his proceedings. "Successful or unsuccessful," he added, "it would not have made the slightest difference in the terms proposed."[73]

Many factors contributed to the successful issue of the Oregon problem. Aberdeen believed that the United States wanted to solve it before the less conciliatory Palmerston returned to the Foreign Office. Everett emphasized that the Southern states feared Britain might make common cause with Mexico if the compromise were rejected. No doubt the repeal of the British Corn Laws, which opened new opportunities for American agricultural exports, played a part in improving feelings between the two nations, and thus aided the settlement.

But Aberdeen would have wanted it to be remembered as a triumph of men of peace and good will, such as Edward Everett, Louis McLane, and himself, over the forces of nationalism and jingoism, and not as a diplomatic victory of one country over the other, which it was not. One can sense the feeling of pride and satisfaction Aberdeen experienced in penning a sentence in his last letter to Pakenham: "On our retirement . . . I am not aware that we leave any question behind us which is likely to grow into a serious quarrel with the United States."[74]

## CHAPTER VI

# Lord Aberdeen: An Estimate

FROM a short study such as this the reader is apt to derive at most a series of fleeting impressions of the personality and mind of the statesman who guided Britain's foreign relations during the period 1841-1846. The whole man, under these circumstances, is not likely to take shape, so perhaps a few lines in conclusion regarding Aberdeen and his policies might therefore be in order.

The intellect with which we come into contact through the medium of Aberdeen's letters is a vigorous one. While he accorded the highest respect to the opinions of his colleagues, Aberdeen insisted that his own be viewed in the same manner. His was also an independent mind. Aberdeen knew what he wanted and did not hesitate to make his superior, Peel, aware of his views.

The personality we meet in the same manner is serious and mild, but not without a strong undercurrent of emotion which provided a stable basis for his outlook. This latter quality was most evident when his policies came under attack either by the Opposition, or other members of the Government. Aberdeen felt he was right even more than he knew he was right. Hence attacks might disturb him momentarily, but in the long run they would merely make him more tenacious in holding to his views.

Certain aspects of his personality are particularly attractive. One is his loyalty to his subordinates, even when their activities caused him and the Government acute embarrassment. Another is his manner of associating with the various statesmen who presented themselves at the Foreign Office. A minister from Texas wrote that Aberdeen received him "very kindly and without any ceremony. . . . I understood the Earl to be a very plain, matter of fact man, entirely free

from ostentation, and almost free from court etiquette. . . ."
Because of his own humility of spirit, Aberdeen displayed
those social qualities, often found among the British aristoc-
racy, which never fail to charm and sometimes captivate
individuals from the republics of the New World.

If Aberdeen himself had been asked to designate his best
quality, he would undoubtedly have answered that it was his
love of peace. This pacifism can perhaps be traced to two
sources. First, during the late Napoleonic period he had
observed first hand the horrors and futility of war. And
second, his pacifism was nourished by his religious feelings,
those of an Anglican who lived in a Presbyterian environment.
The theological stress of the latter on Original Sin and the
depraved nature of man left a strong imprint on Aberdeen's
thought and general outlook.

Because he believed mankind to be inherently depraved,
Aberdeen could not be a complete pacifist. War, indeed,
was the worst of crimes, yet because human society is so
imperfect, even war might be necessary at times to serve
some noble purpose or to protect the vital interests of the
state. But if war were resorted to, it should be looked upon
as the most disagreeable of necessities, wholly devoid of the
glorious qualities some statesmen have tried to attach to it.
His record of opposition to war speaks for itself.

Aberdeen's convictions regarding the imperfections of
man and society caused him to play the game of diplomacy
according to the rules of necessity. Thus, if bribery were
necessary, Aberdeen would resort to it. If playing a "bluff"
were necessary, he would try that also. The first of these
means we have noted in the Maine boundary controversy;
the second, in the La Plata. Both in his written and spoken
communications Aberdeen, when this seemed necessary, inter-
larded his promises with loopholes through which, if need
be, he might retire gracefully. One instance of this was in
his interview with Abrantes in late 1844, and another was his
conference with Murphy earlier the same year.

But if Aberdeen used such means on occasion, it does
not follow that they had the stamp of his approval, or that
he believed diplomacy should be carried on in this way. In

cases where openness was met with openness, Aberdeen virtually let down all the bars. It is said that he showed his instructions and even private letters to Guizot; there can be little doubt that he was almost as frank with Everett and McLane. Nothing pleased him more than to work with an individual of sound common sense and pacific disposition from a foreign nation, and he liked to think that they reflected similar qualities in the countries they represented. In this respect Aberdeen seems to have had the most confidence in the United States, possibly for reasons of kinship, and somewhat less with regard to the French people. For those of the Latin American culture he always retained doubts and suspicions.

While these observations may imperfectly describe Aberdeen as a personality, they do nothing to answer a question of deep interest to the historian—how successful was he as a Foreign Secretary? Often he is presented as a sort of peace-loving non-entity who could be bluffed and badgered into making almost any sort of concession. While most writers credit him with having high principles, few emphasize his technical ability as a diplomat.

Most of those who have reached these conclusions judge Lord Aberdeen on the basis of his tactics rather than his grand strategy. They point out that he compromised Britain's claims in Maine, permitted an apology in the *Caroline* case, allowed himself to be hoodwinked in the matter of the cruising convention, gave up the Columbia River boundary in the Oregon affair, failed to prevent either the annexation of Texas or the Mexican War, and involved his country in an unsuccessful invasion of the La Plata.

If one judges Aberdeen on these bases, then his administration of foreign affairs was indeed a failure. But when one does so, he must conclude that the areas he compromised away, the apology he gave, and the annexation he failed to prevent were of vital interest to Britain. All sorts of reasons may be unearthed to give substance to this point of view. Yet were these things really vital to Britain? Aberdeen obviously did not think so, and it must be pointed out that he was deeply patriotic and wholly attached to the interests of his nation.

Aberdeen's success or failure should be determined on the basis of his grand strategy, and this, in turn, must be judged from a long range point of view. Aberdeen's influence extended far beyond his term of office or connection in any way with the Government. His views were deeply impressed upon two men at least—Lord Stanley, who, later as Lord Derby, was three times Prime Minister, and William Ewart Gladstone, who succeeded to the leadership of the Liberals. So long as Derby lived the pacific policies of Aberdeen were characteristic of the Conservative Party; after his death, and the succession of Disraeli, these policies passed to Gladstone and the Liberal Party. During the Cabinet sessions and governmental intercourse of the period 1841-1846, Aberdeen profoundly influenced the outlook of these two men.

Viewed in this light, the fate of Aberdeen's grand strategy may be traced into the several decades after the fall of Peel. While it is true that Britain's relations with France turned for the worse shortly after Aberdeen retired as Foreign Secretary, this condition was not long-lived. The Derby Administration of 1852 took up the policy of friendship with France, and during Aberdeen's Administration which succeeded it the two countries, of course, were allies in the Crimean War. France also cooperated with Britain in the second war with China, 1858-1860, and Gladstone's commercial treaty with France of 1860 was in the Aberdeen tradition. While it is true that colonial differences caused tension between the two nations later in the century, the traditional hostility between the two nations appears to have been buried by Aberdeen and Guizot, whose work foreshadowed the entente of 1904.

A second major policy was winning the friendship of the United States. Obviously the two nations did not become allies as a result of Aberdeen's compromises, but there was much truth in his observation that he left little of an important nature for them to quarrel over. During the Derby Administrations, and especially during the American Civil War,[1] the Conservative Party inherited the Aberdeen tradition, and pursued a correct, if not always enthusiastically friendly, attitude toward the United States. While Gladstone showed partisanship toward the South during the War Between the States, it was his famous arbitration of the Alabama Claims in 1871 which opened a new era of good feeling between the United States and Britain.

How successful was Aberdeen's endeavor to split the United States and France? Certainly as a result of his activities American relations with Britain were much improved, while those between France and the United States took a turn for the worse. It may well be that the Palmerston Government had Aberdeen's policy in mind when they involved Britain in the triple intervention in Mexico in 1861, and then left France alone to become the object of American post-war spleen. But this writer has not made a study of that important incident. At any rate, Aberdeen's policy of splitting the two countries looked definitely toward the future, and few will deny that the American intervention in the two World Wars was prompted more by the desire to aid Britain than to pay a debt to Lafayette.

# Notes

## CHAPTER I

1. In 1840 Palmerston had sponsored a convention for the pacification of the Levant with Russia, Prussia, and Austria, and had excluded France. This caused such resentment in France that the King, to avoid war, replaced his minister, Adolphe Thiers, with Francois Guizot. Instead of conciliating the new government, Palmerston snubbed Guizot by failing to mention France in the Queen's Speech of 1841.
2. The *Caroline* was an American ship which had been supplying the rebels in Canada. On December 29, 1837 a band of British volunteers sank the ship in New York waters. One American was killed during the incident, and this was the basis of the murder charge against McLeod.
3. This was in the case of Portugal. "You may be as close-fisted as ever you please towards France, Russia, Naples & even Spain without a word of remonstrance from me," Aberdeen wrote Ripon in 1842. "But I really consider our relations with Portugal as of a character entirely different from those of any other country. The Tagus is by far the most important spot in Europe for us, out of our own Dominions, and I therefore wish that we should not only be Masters there, but at home there. AP 43072, Aberdeen to Ripon, December 14, 1842.
4. "We are terribly hampered by this Slave Trade," Aberdeen complained in 1844, "the questions about which meet us in every quarter & estrange us from our best friends. France, the U. States, Spain, Portugal, Brazil, all furnish matter for angry discussions every day. Never [have] a people made such a sacrifice as we have done to attain our object, & the payment of the money is the least part of it. We must not relax: but our progress has not been hitherto very encouraging." AP 43064. Aberdeen to Peel, October 8, 1844.
5. *See*: PP 40497. Peel's Memorandum on England and America, December 1841, and Ripon's Minute on World Trade, 1841. Britain's colonies accounted for only 25% of her total trade. The declared value of British exports to the United States reached a high - £12,500,000 in 1836, but slumped to £6,750,000 in 1840. ". . . the British Interests there involved are of great magnitude," Peel concluded. At the moment they regarded American tariff policies as "restrictive," but not prohibitory. In December, 1941, in the hope of finding some way of restoring the high level of the American trade, the Cabinet discussed Lord Ashburton's suggestion to give preferential rates to American corn. On the other hand, France, Russia, and Spain followed prohibitory policies. Much of Britain's trade with France was the work of smugglers, who, Peel noted,

provided "a sort of safety valve for Commerce" between those nations.

6. AP 43072. Ripon to Aberdeen, September 14, 1841.

7. There is, however, an interesting note in Aberdeen's book of excerpts from Mexico under date of January 31, 1842. On January 13, 1842 Hamilton offered Santa Anna a $5,000,000 "indemnity" in exchange for the recognition of Texas, transmitting the proposal through the British minister in Mexico. Aberdeen wrote: "Mr. Pakenham unconsciously is made the channel through wh. General Hamilton delivers a letter to Santa Anna, offering him besides the 5 millions dollars, 200,000 as a present for the recognition of the independence of Texas." AP 43170. (From Mexico, January 31, 1842.) The phrase "the 5 millions" hints that Aberdeen may have been familiar with the plan. After Santa Anna rejected the offer (as being too small), Aberdeen complained to the representative of Texas in London that the transmittal of such a letter through the British minister had been "quite improper," and he was told that the government of Texas had had nothing to do with the proposal.

## CHAPTER II

1. Charles S. Parker, *Sir Robert Peel* (London: John Murray, 1899), II, 462, 492. Wellington to Peel, May 17, 1841; Graham to Peel, August 1, 1841.

2. *Ibid.*, III, 387-388. Peel's Memorandum, October 17, 1841.

3. A cargo of slaves seized control of this American ship, which was conveying them to New Orleans, and brought it to the Bahamas, where they received their freedom.

4. In his anxiety to assure Ashburton's success, Aberdeen almost wrecked the negotiation. On December 20, 1841 he drew up an exposition of the British views regarding the right of "visit"(*See*: Executive Documents, 27th Congress, 3rd Session, Vol. 422, pp. 7-10. Aberdeen to Everett, December 20, 1841), and he instructed Fox to publish it in a newspaper without delay. Finding that the President did not approve of its publication, Fox tactfully disobeyed instructions. AP 43123. Aberdeen to Fox; Fox to Aberdeen, April 27, 1842.

5. Aberdeen Memorandum, February 14, 1842.

6. Aberdeen to Ashburton, March 3, 1842.

7. Wellington Memorandum, February 8, 1842.

8. Aberdeen to Ashburton, February 9, 1842.

9. Aberdeen Memorandum, February 14, 1842.

10. Aberdeen to Ashburton, May 16, 20, 1842.

11. *See*: E. D. Adams, "Lord Ashburton and the Treaty of Washington," *American Historical Review* (New York), XVII (July, 1912), 764-782, and J. R. Baldwin, "The Ashburton-Webster Boundary Settlement," Canadian Historical Association, *Report of the Annual Meeting, May, 1938* (Toronto, 1938), 121-133. The present writer revised Adams' findings in "Lord Ashburton and the Maine Boundary Negotiations," *The Mississippi Valley Historical Review*, XL (December, 1953), 477-490, and in "The Influence of Slavery on the Webster-Ashburton Negotiations," *The Journal of Southern History*, XXII (February, 1956), 48-58.

12. AP 43123. Aberdeen to Ashburton, July 2, 1842.
13. *Ibid.*
14. Aberdeen to Ashburton, September 26, 1842.
15. AP 43063. Ashburton to Croker, January ?, 1844.
16. Peel to Aberdeen, January 27, 1844.
17. PP 40507. Memorandum, April 26, 1842.
18. The Lizardi Company appears occasionally in the correspondence, and its activities are of considerable interest. The British minister in Mexico reported early in 1844 that Santa Anna and the Ministers of War, Finance, Justice and Foreign Affairs had all received bribes from that concern ranging from $2,000 to $18,000. "This will prove... ," he wrote, "the extreme difficulty of getting any measure of justice to the Bond-holders carried through, that is to say, as long as Messrs. Lizardi and Company can afford to continue their system of bribery and General Santa Anna remains in power." AP 43126. Doyle to Aberdeen, January 29, 1844.
19. *See*: E. D. Adams, *British Interests and Activities in Texas* (Baltimore: The Johns Hopkins Press, 1910), 83-96.
20. Ashburton explained the British position to President Tyler, and he seemed "satisfied." AP 43126. Ashburton to Aberdeen, July 13, 1842. Aberdeen wrote Elliot: ". . . you must do what you can to deprive the proceedings of any hostile character." Aberdeen to Elliot, December 3, 1842.
21. *Annual Report of the American Historical Association, 1908.* (Washington, 1911), II, 960-961. Smith to Jones, June 3, 1842.
22. "The Mexican return of Imports," wrote Peel, "is so confirmatory of our loss of that Market, by the French & German competition in the *Fine Cloths* . . . as to require the earliest consideration." RP 40863. Peel to Ripon, July 16, 1842.
23. Elliot to Aberdeen, September 15, 1842.
24. AP 43170. From Mexico, August 29, 1842.
25. From Mexico, December 25, 1842. Waddy Thompson was the American Minister in Mexico.
26. On this point *see*: Justin H. Smith, *The Annexation of Texas* (Barnes & Noble, Inc., 1941), 84-85.
27. AP 43170. To Mexico, July 15, 1842.
28. AP 43126. Aberdeen to Elliot, December 3, 1842.
29. AP 43170. From Mexico, February 24, 1843.
30. From Mexico, March 23, 1843.
31. AP 43126. Doyle to Aberdeen, April 24, 1843.
32. AP 43170. From Mexico, May 25, 1843.
33. AP 43126. Doyle to Aberdeen, July 30, 1843.
34. *Ibid.*
35. *Annual Report*, 1908, III, 1090-1091. Elliot to Jones, June 10, 1842.

## CHAPTER III

1. *Hansard* (third series), LXXX, 232-233.
2. AP 43123. Ashburton to Aberdeen, January 1, 1843.
3. AP 43170. From Mexico, January 6, 1842.

4. COP, CO 43/100. Hope to Canning, November 23, 1841.
5. RP 40864. Peel to Ripon, April 24, 1843.
6. AP 43123. Ashburton to Aberdeen, January 1, 1843.
7. Ashburton to Aberdeen, January 6, 1843.
8. Ashburton to Aberdeen, January 1, 1843. Ashburton's instructions had insisted on the extreme British claim, including the entire area north and west of the Columbia River from its mouth to its intersection with the 49th degree parallel.
9. Everett to Aberdeen, November 1, 1843.
10. "I am unfeignedly at your service," Ashburton wrote, ". . . always excepting the undertaking a second journey across the Atlantic, or attempting to settle your differences at Pekin." Ashburton to Aberdeen, October 27, 1842.
11. Aberdeen to Pakenham, October 7, 1843.
12. Aberdeen to Fox, November 2, 1843.
13. Everett to Aberdeen, November 30, 1843.
14. Aberdeen to Pakenham, March 4, 1844.
15. "I believe," wrote Aberdeen, "that if the line of the 49th degree were extended only to the water's edge, and should leave us possession of all Vancouver's Island, with the Northern side of the entrance to Puget's Sound; and if all the Harbours within the Sound, and to the Columbia, inclusive, were made free to both Countries, and further if the River Columbia from the point at which it became navigable to its mouth, were also made free to both, this would be in reality a most advantageous settlement. . . . I am convinced that this is the utmost which can be hoped for from the negotiation." AP 43064. Aberdeen to Peel, September 25, 1844.
16. Samuel Flagg Bemis, ed., *The American Secretaries of State and Their Diplomacy* (New York: Alfred A. Knopf, 1928), V, 120-121.
17. Ibid., 197.
18. One British representative in Texas reported: "The promotors of it [the abolition convention] all had gain for their purpose, and some hoped to replenish their pockets out of the over-flowing coffers of John Bull, others to excite the interest of the United States in Texas. Mr. Thomas League, the abolition associate of Mr. Andrews (who waited once in London), on being charged in Galveston with being an abolitionist denied it saying '. . . all he wanted was to get one thousand dollars a piece for his own slaves from the British Government . . . and then pass them across the Sabine to the States, and sell them again'." AP 43126. Kennedy to Aberdeen, May 10, 1844.
19. Santa Anna's attitude was described by Doyle, who heard him say that he regretted not having slaves for his own farms, which were "very large but yield no rent for want of hands to work the land." Doyle to Aberdeen, November 29, 1843.
20. Doyle to Aberdeen, July 30, 1843.
21. "With respect to the Copper Decree," Doyle wrote, "the history of its being issued is simply that some persons who have weight with Santa Anna have speculated in the certificates and a friend of mine took him on its being issued 25,000 dollars. The decree has however done some good to the persons interested." Doyle to Aberdeen, December 30, 1843. Under the provisions of this decree the devaluated copper was called in and replaced by a stable currency.

22. Doyle to Aberdeen, October 30, 1843; December 30, 1843.
23. Statistics for the War of 1812 are not very complete, and sometimes conflict. Lloyd's listed five hundred British merchantmen and three frigates captured by the Americans in seven months. One authority believes that a list of $9,507,000 worth of British ships and goods sold at auction by privateers and navy vessels represents only a third of the actual total. Hundreds of American vessels operated during the war, some in the vicinity of the British Isles. *See*: Fletcher Pratt. *The Navy* (Garden City Publishing Co., 1941).
24. Smith, *Annexation of Texas*, 382-406.
25. *Ibid.*, 394.
26. Ephraim D. Adams, *British Interests and Activities in Texas, 1838-1846* (Baltimore: The Johns Hopkins Press, 1910), 171-172.
27. PP 40454. Peel to Aberdeen, May 26. 1844.
28. AP 43064. Aberdeen to Peel, September 23, 1845.
29. Aberdeen to Peel, January 31, 1845.
30. In the opinion of this writer diplomatic considerations so far overshadowed those of an economic nature in Aberdeen's mind that to emphasize the latter beclouds the issue. "To Great Britain," Aberdeen wrote late in 1844, "it is of comparatively minor consequence in the abstract, and apart from considerations connected with the interests of Mexico, whether Texas be independent, or whether she be annexed to the United States. Texas is of importance to Great Britain principally in a commercial point of view, but annexed to the U. S., Texas wd. probably be scarcely less productive of advantage in that particular, than if she remained independent." AP 43170. To Mexico, December 31, 1844.
31. Aberdeen, in fact, granted sick leave to his only capable assistant in Texas that spring, and had at Galveston only a Mr. Kennedy whose health "not merely bodily, but I fear mental, has given way under the effects of strong drink." AP 43126 Elliot to Aberdeen, March ?, 1844.
32. *See*: Smith, *Annexation of Texas*, 389-390 and footnote 14. This authority calls the qualifying phrases "prudent reserve." As Guizot would be likely to follow Aberdeen's wishes, the latter could use an alleged French change of attitude to back out whenever he so desired.
33. *See*: COP, PRO 43/104 (Stephen to Addington, May 22, 1844), and PP 40468 (Stanley to Peel, September 5, 1844; Peel to Stanley, September 7, 1844; Stanley to Peel, August 18, 1845). The Canadians, however, were encouraged to organize their own defenses.
34. PP 40454. Peel to Aberdeen, August 21, 1844.
35. Aberdeen to Peel, August 22, 1844.
36. Aberdeen to Peel, August 21, 1844.
37. PP 40468. Peel to Stanley, November 7, 1844; Stanley to Peel, November 11, 1844.
38. AP 43064. Aberdeen to Peel, December 4, 1844.
39. Aberdeen to Peel, January 31, 1845.

## CHAPTER IV

1. *Hansard* (third series), LXXXIII, 1159.
2. AP 43123. Aberdeen to Ashburton, July 2, 1842.

3. GP 44285. Ripon to Gladstone, October 14, 1841.
4. AP 43072. Ripon to Aberdeen, April 24, 1843.
5. AP 43064. Aberdeen to Peel, November 25, 1843.
6. Peel to Aberdeen, November 26, 1843.
7. Aberdeen to Peel, November 27, 1843.
8. Aberdeen to Peel, October 18, 1844.
9. Aberdeen to Peel, October 21, 1844.
10. Aberdeen to Peel, December 25, 1845.
11. Aberdeen to Peel, December 4, 1844.
12. AP 43127. Ouseley to Aberdeen, January 10, 1845.
13. *Ibid.*
14. As we have seen, Aberdeen feared that Brazilian troops, once ensconced in Montevideo, might be as difficult to remove as those from Buenos Aires then operating in Uruguay. The cavalier treatment of Brazil, however, perhaps indicates the existence of an opinion in the Peel Cabinet of hostility and dislike of that slave-holding nation. The climax of this sequence of events was reached in August 1845 when Parliament passed the "Aberdeen Act," which permitted British ships to seize Brazilian slavers and to try such captures in Admiralty or Vice-Admiralty Courts, even though the Anglo-Brazilian treaty on the subject had expired. Britain contended that Article I of their treaty of 1826 was perpetual. One of Aberdeen's biographers rightly describes this action as "high-handed." *See:* Sir Arthur Gordon, *The Earl of Aberdeen* (New York: Harper & Brothers, 1893), 184-185.
15. AP 43064. Aberdeen to Peel, September 23, 1845.
16. AP 43127. Ouseley to Aberdeen, April 21, 1845. The following year Secretary of State Buchanan wrote William A. Harris, the new American Minister at Buenos Aires that Britain and France had "flagrantly violated" the principle of non-interference recently alluded to in Polk's address by their intervention in the La Plata. He explained that "existing circumstances" prevented the United States from intervening in the dispute, but that the United States cordially wished for the success of Argentina. Thus, Brent's acts received a sort of *ex post facto* support by his Government, even though his activities were disavowed at the time. This incident is discussed authoritatively in: Samuel Flagg Bemis, *The Latin American Policy of the United States* (New York: Harcourt, Brace and Company, 1943), 100-102. Bemis, however, perhaps underestimates the effects of Brent's interference.
17. AP 43127. Ouseley to Aberdeen, April 21, 1845.
18. Ouseley to Pakenham, April 20, 1845.
19. Ouseley to Aberdeen, May 29, 1845.
20. *Ibid.*
21. Ouseley to Aberdeen, August 13, 1845.
22. *Ibid.*
23. Rosas' reply to this, Ouseley complained, was "coarsely abusive in tone." Ouseley to Aberdeen, December 21, 1845.
24. Ouseley to Aberdeen, September 8, 1845.
25. Ouseley to Aberdeen, September 9, 1845.
26. "Thus it is that I proposed the Parana expedition . . .," Ouseley wrote, but later: "Besides was I to separate myself on this important point from my colleague?" Ouseley to Aberdeen, January 24 and June 6, 1846.

27. "The Enemy's works were admirably constructed—all the Engineering good. The Guns, firing etc. excellent—the officers said this must have been the works of Europeans & that some English were there—I hope they were Americans—& the engineering & money were given it is said by another nation. 11 Englishmen gave themselves up, saying that they were forced to serve." Ouseley to Aberdeen, Novmber 30, 1845. The writer has no information on the implied charge against the United States.
28. *Ibid.*
29. Ouseley to Aberdeen, December 22, 1845.
30. Ouseley to Aberdeen, January 24, 1846.
31. *Hansard* (third series), LXXVII, 169-170.
32. *Ibid.*, LXXXI, 1307.
33. AP 43064. Aberdeen to Peel, September 17, 1845.
34. Aberdeen to Peel, September 23, 1845.
35. AP 43127. Aberdeen to Ouseley, October 8, 1845.
36. Ouseley to Aberdeen, January 31, 1846.
37. Ouseley to Aberdeen, June 6, 1846—Confidential Memorandum, July 4, 1846. "It must be admitted," Ouseley concluded, "that they [Rosas' fabrications] are continued with a perseverence, talent and unhappily, success, that is truly wonderful, and were it employed in a good cause, would excite admiration."
38. On November 3 Stanley wrote Peel: "I foresee that this question, if you persevere in your present opinion, must break up the Government. . ." PP 40468. Stanley to Peel, November 3, 1845. From that day on the end of the Peel Government was in sight.
39. AP 43127. Aberdeen to Ouseley, December 3, 1845.
40. AP 43065. Aberdeen to Peel, December 25, 1845.
41. AP 43127. Aberdeen to Ouseley, December 27, 1845.
42. Aberdeen to Ouseley, March 4, 1846.
43. Aberdeen to Ouseley 8, 1846.
44. AP 43065. Peel to Aberdeen, April 12, 1846.
45. Aberdeen to Peel, April 14, 1846.
46. AP 43127. Aberdeen to Ouseley, July 2, 1846.
47. Confidential Memorandum, July 4, 1846. This memorial is largely a rehash of Ouseley's private letters to Aberdeen. Included also in the correspondence are Ouseley's letters regarding the Hood mission, received after Aberdeen was out of office. There are also two letters to Aberdeen written in 1848, at which time Ouseley was seeking to remove the stigma of the censure and to secure employment under Palmerston.
48. Aberdeen to Ouseley, May 19, 1846.

## CHAPTER V

1. AP 43064. Aberdeen to Peel, October 21, 1844.
2. Frederick Merk, an American scholar who spent more time studying the Oregon crisis in recent years than any other, reached quite an opposite conclusion. He notes that Aberdeen feared attacks by Palmerston if he made a compromise settlement in Oregon, and notes that

British party politics "induced the British government to postpone a settlement until passions had been aroused in the United States almost to a point of explosion." Frederick Merk, "British Party Politics and the Oregon Treaty," *The American Historical Review*, XXXVII (1932), 677. While due weight must be given to any of Professor Merk's statements on this subject, the present writer must record a decided dissent from this interpretation, involving, as it does, a slur.

3. AP 43064. Peel to Aberdeen, February 23, 1845.
4. *Hansard* (third series), LXXX, 236-237.
5. AP 43064. Aberdeen to Peel, March 29, 1845.
6. AP 43123. Aberdeen to Pakenham, April 2, 1845.
7. *Hansard* (third series), LXXIX, 193-199.
8. *Ibid.*, pp. 120-123.
9. Frederick Merk, "British Government Propaganda and the Oregon Treaty," *The American Historical Review*, XL (1934), 39.
10. It will be noted that both Peel and Aberdeen were impressed by Polk's phrase "clear and unquestionable." Aberdeen, in fact, asked Everett where the President got it. Everett was unable to say immediately, but later reported that it appeared in a resolution of the Baltimore Convention of May 1844. AP 43123. Everett to Aberdeen, July 30, 1846.
11. Aberdeen to Pakenham, April 18, 1845.
12. AP 43065. Peel to Aberdeen, October 2, 1845.
13. Aberdeen to Peel, October 3, 1845.
14. AP 43123. Aberdeen to Pakenham, October 3, 1845.
15. AP 43065. Peel to Aberdeen, November 22, 1845.
16. AP 43123. Gratton to Aberdeen, September 30 and November 16, 1844. Gratton, the British consul in Boston, proved to be a remarkable election prognosticator.
17. AP 43126. Jones to Elliot, February 16, 1845. An extract only.
18. Elliot to Aberdeen, February 24, 1845.
19. "The removal from Texas of the American agent may be a pretext with the United States for direct hostility against Texas," Peel wrote. AP 43064. Peel to Aberdeen, February 23, 1845. A strange line of thought, indeed, at a time when the United States was in the process of annexing Texas.
20. AP 43064. Peel to Aberdeen, May 12, 1845.
21. AP 43126. Elliot to Aberdeen, May 23, 1845.
22. AP 43123. Aberdeen to Pakenham, April 2, 1845.
23. AP 43170. To Mexico, May 15 and May 31, 1845.
24. AP 43064. Peel to Aberdeen, May 12, 1845.
25. AP 43126. Terrell to Aberdeen, June 2, 1845.
26. Aberdeen to Terrell, June 3, 1845.
27. Louis Philippe wanted Queen Isabella of Spain or her sister to marry someone from the House of Bourbon; Aberdeen considered this would be a breach of the Treaty of Utrecht. While Aberdeen was at the Foreign Office, however, this did not become a serious issue.
28. AP 43064. Peel to Aberdeen, September 18, 1845.
29. Aberdeen to Peel, September 18, 1845.
30. AP 43170. To Mexico, October 23, 1844.
31. To Mexico, December 31, 1844.
32. To Mexico, May 31, 1845.

33. AP 43126. Bankhead to Aberdeen, July 30, 1845.
34. AP 43064. Aberdeen to Peel, September 23, 1845. Aberdeen also mentions in this letter that Britain had been offered California that spring, and that "we might have established our *Protectorate* long ago, if we had thought proper." No other details are given.
35. *Ibid*. This document quite obviously strengthens the American position with respect to the origins of the Mexican War, and the others in the series have the same tendency.
36. Peel to Aberdeen, September 24, 1845.
37. Aberdeen to Peel, September 25, 1845.
38. Aberdeen to Peel, October 3, 1845.
39. AP 43170. To Mexico, October 1, 1845.
40. AP 43065. Peel to Aberdeen, November 14, 1845.
41. Aberdeen to Peel, October 11, 1845.
42. PP 40455. Peel to Aberdeen, October 17, 1845.
43. AP 43065. Aberdeen to Peel, October 20, 1845.
44. Aberdeen to Peel, October 21, 1845.
45. Aberdeen to Peel, November 27, 1845.
46. Peel to Aberdeen, November 27, 1845.
47. Aberdeen to Peel, December 29, 1845.
48. AP 43123. Pakenham to Aberdeen, May 28, 1846.
49. AP 43126. Bankhead to Aberdeen, May 31, 1846.
50. AP 43170. To Mexico, June 1, 1846.
51. AP 43064. Aberdeen to Peel, August 25, 1845.
52. *Ibid*. Aberdeen seems to have intentionally minimized the extent of the American claim. *See*: Bemis, *American Secretaries*, V, 256-257.
53. AP 43064. Aberdeen to Peel, September 17, 1845.
54. Aberdeen to Peel, November 21, 1845.
55. Peel to Aberdeen, December 3, 1845.
56. AP 43123. Aberdeen to Pakenham, December 3, 1845.
57. AP 43065. Peel to Aberdeen, December 26, 1845.
58. Parker, *Peel*, III, 324. Peel to Egerton, January 6, 1846.
59. RP 40874. Ripon to Hardinge, December 24, 1845.
60. AP 43065. Aberdeen to Peel, December 25, 1845.
61. Frederick Merk in his article on British Government Propaganda, cited above, shows that Aberdeen inspired an editorial of January 3, 1846 in *The Times*, which changed sharply the attitude of that influential newspaper from one of hostility toward the United States to one of conciliation. He states that this change gave "respectability and standing" to a British policy of concession. H. C. Allen in *Great Britain and the United States* (New York: St. Martin's Press, 1955), 413, also strongly emphasizes the influence of this editorial. While a conciliatory press in Britain helped Aberdeen, his chief worry was the American, not the British attitude. The above warning to Everett, incidentally, was written the same day that editorial appeared.
62. AP 43123. Aberdeen to Everett, January 3, 1846.
63. Everett to Aberdeen, January 28, 1846. Aberdeen must have received Pakenham's letter of December 29, 1845, in which he charged that Everett had convinced the American Government that Aberdeen would accept "almost any terms" to end the controversy, about the middle of January, and this may have helped convince Aberdeen that a

stronger stand was necessary to break the deadlock.

64. Frederick Merk in his article on British party politics, cited above, emphasizes the part played by these letters in bringing about the settlement. In the opinion of the present writer the attitude of the Opposition played little part. Aberdeen was ready in September, 1844 to make the final compromise, but, as we have seen, the attitude of the American Government discouraged it. Calhoun's statement of 1844 that the United States Senate would not accept less than the 49th parallel was, in effect, a rejection of the compromise.

65. Aberdeen to Pakenham, February 3, 1846.

66. McLane to Aberdeen, March 17, 1846, enclosing extract.

67. RP 40875. Ripon to Hardinge, February 7, 1846.

68. *See*: Wilbur D. Jones and J. Chal Vinson, "British Preparedness and the Oregon Settlement," *The Pacific Historical Review*, XXII (1953), 353-364. Professor Vinson, whose field is American diplomatic history, shares this view with the present writer. For an opposing view, *see*: Henry C. Commager, "England and the Oregon Treaty, 1846," *Oregon Historical Quarterly*, XXVIII (1927), 38.

69. AP 43123. Aberdeen to Pakenham, May 18, 1846.

70. *See*: Bemis, *American Secretaries*, V. 261-262.

71. AP 43123. Aberdeen to Pakenham, May 18, 1846.

72. Pakenham to Aberdeen, June 7, 1846.

73. Aberdeen to Pakenham, June 30, 1846.

74. *Ibid.*

## CHAPTER VI

1. This writer has examined in some detail the attitude of the Conservative Party toward the Civil War in: "The British Conservatives and the American Civil War," *The American Historical Review*, LVIII (1953), 527-543.

# Index

Abd-el-Kader Rebellion, 37

Aberdeen, George Hamilton-Gordon, 4th Earl of, early life, ix-x; family life, xi; comes to office, 1; relations with Cabinet, 2-7; friendship with France, 7; attitude toward Texas (1841), 8-9; rejects Hamilton's proposals, 8; projects Ashburton mission, 10-11; concessions to the United States, 11-13; opinion of Webster-Ashburton Treaty, 14; sponsors Quintuple Treaty, 15; basic policies toward France and the United States, 15; first intervention in Texas, 17; second intervention in Texas, 18-24; rejects California projects, 26; accepts Ashburton's advice, 26-27; appoints Pakenham to Washington, 28; and the Diplomatic Act, 31-37; resists preparedness program, 37-39; intervention in La Plata, 40-55; and Oregon, 56-62; speech on Oregon, 60-61; accepts Colorado River boundary, 63; loses interest in Texas, 63; explains Mexico's attitude, 65; resigns, 67; adopts non-interference policy, 67; considers offer of California, 68-71; policy toward Mexican War, 71-76; policy toward France and America, 71, 74; and "Rough Rice" question, 76-77; seeks to arbitrate Oregon dispute, 77-79; threat of force, 79-81; satisfaction at time of resignation, 82; personality, 83-84; nature of his pacifism, 84; methods of diplomacy 84-85; superficial aspects of his diplomacy, 85; success of his principles, 86-87.

Abrantes, Viscount, 42-44

Adams, Ephraim D., 34

Aden, 78

Alabama Claims, 87

Albert, Prince Consort, 31

Algeria, 37

America, United States of, and Maine boundary, 10-15; expansion, 17-18; offers mediation in Texas, 20; opposes emancipation, 20; treaty with Texas, 21-22; and Oregon (1843-1844), 25-31; and the Diplomatic Act, 32-37; remonstrance to Brazil, 40; ignores agreement, 41; opposes Britain and France in La Plata, 45; and Oregon, 56-62, 77-82; annexes Texas, 62-66; war with Mexico, 75

Ashburton, Alexander Baring, 1st Lord, introduces Hamilton, 7; undertakes Maine boundary negotiations, 11-13; and minor problems, 13-14; rejects honors, 14; regarding his treaty, 14; and "right of visit," 25; distrusts American administration, 27. Mentioned, 28-29, 40-41

Banda Oriental, 45, 47, 51

Bankhead, Charles, appointment, 32; advises mediation, 68; seeks California, 68; suggests triple intervention in Mexico, 74-75. Mentioned, 67, 71

Beaconsfield, Benjamin Disraeli, 1st Earl of, adopts Palmerston's policies, 86

Bolivia, 48

Brazil, and trade with Britain, 40-41; invites intervention in La Plata, 42-43; ignored, 43; offended, 45. Mentioned, 2, 93 (f. 16)

Brent, William, Jr., opposes Anglo-French intervention in La Plata, 45

Buchanan, James, offers compromise,